LANGUAGE IN SOCIETY 8

Language, the Sexes and Society

LANGUAGE IN SOCIETY

GENERAL EDITOR
Peter Trudgill, Professor of Linguistic Science,
University of Reading

ADVISORY EDITORS
Ralph Fasold, Professor of Linguistics,
Georgetown University
William Labov, Professor of Linguistics,
University of Pennsylvania

Language, the Sexes and Society

PHILIP M. SMITH

BASIL BLACKWELL

Basil Blackwell Publisher Ltd
108 Cowley Road, Oxford OX4 1JF, UK

Basil Blackwell Inc.
432 Park Avenue South, Suite 1505,
New York, NY 10016, USA

British Library Cataloguing in Publication Data

Smith, Philip M.
    Language, the sexes and society. – (Language in society; 8)
    1. Language and languages – Sex differences
    1. Title   II. Series
    418   P120.S48

    ISBN 0-631-11111-5
    ISBN 0-631-12753–4 Pbk

Library of Congress Cataloging in Publication Data

Smith, Philip M., 1953–
    Language, the sexes and society.

    (Language in society ; 8)
    Bibliography: p. 182
    Including indexes.
    1. Language and Languages – Sex differences.
    2. Sociolinguistics. I. Title.
    II. Series: Language in society (Oxford, Oxfordshire) ; 8.
    P120.S48S54   1985   401'.9   84-14489
    ISBN 0-631-11111-5
    ISBN 0-631-12753-4 (pbk.)

Typeset by Banbury Typesetters Ltd, Banbury, Oxfordshire
Printed in Great Britain by Redwood Burn Ltd, Trowbridge, Wiltshire

To Sharon

Contents

Editor's Preface

The study of the relationship between language and sex is by no means new. During the course of this century, works have appeared every now and then that have dealt, at least in part, with this subject, or have mentioned it in passing. In the last two decades, however, there has been an enormous upsurge of interest, and literally thousands of papers and articles have been written on different aspects of the subject. Some have been insightful, informative, thought-provoking, scholarly and exciting. Very many of them have been none of these things. Few writers, however, have accorded this topic the excellent in-depth, book-length treatment that Philip Smith has given it in this volume.

The linguistic study of language and sex has not been free from controversy, which is, of course, typical in investigations where social change is involved: much of the increase of interest in the subject has been related to the contemporary growth of the feminist movement, and a corresponding growing awareness of phenomena such as sexism and sex-role stereotyping. The study of language and sex has focused on a number of different issues, including sexism in language, but also including differences in the use of language and conversational strategies on the part of men and women, as well as dialect and accent differences of a mainly quantitative sort.

In this pioneering work, Philip Smith takes a cool, careful look at all aspects of this research, adding a wealth of original data, insight and interpretation, but concentrating for the most part on attitudinal, social psychological facets of the language behaviour of women and men, and on the origins and causes of what differences there are. Everyone with an interest in the subject of sex and language, whether from the point of view of the psychologist, anthropologist, sociologist, linguist, or simply concerned human being, will find this book highly relevant, challenging and, if my own experience is anything to go by, fascinating.

Peter Trudgill

Acknowledgements

This book has had a long gestation since it was conceived in Bristol in 1978, with the special encouragement of Howard Giles, and the support of series editor Peter Trudgill and John Davey of Basil Blackwell. Conferences in France, England, Sweden, the United States and Canada provided opportunities to make the acquaintance of a long list of people who have been most generous with their help during my research, especially Cheris Kramarae. This work could not have been completed without the financial support of the Social Sciences and Humanities Research Council of Canada during my research at the University of Bristol, and subsequently at the University of British Columbia. I am grateful to John Davey for his patience and constant encouragement even when the tumult threatened to drown the music. Finally, I would like to add my name to the very long list of people who owe an intellectual and spiritual debt to Henri Tajfel, and to the stable of gifted students and colleagues who worked with him at Bristol between 1975 and 1981.

1

Major Influences on Language and Sex Research

Several years ago a well-known feminist author was interviewed on British television about her new book on language and the sexes, in which she argued forcefully that language is a man-made product, designed by and for the male half of the species to the neglect and exclusion of women. Her interviewers, besides the male programme host, were three male academics, two of them full professors of English. I had read her book myself, and was keenly interested in what she had to say as I was in the early stages of writing this book. I was to be surprised and disappointed, however, for the great majority of the words uttered in the 15-minute interview were spoken by the men. In fact, although I did not take accurate measures, I estimated at the time that the author spoke for less than her 'democratic' share of 3 minutes, *much* less than one might have expected under the circumstances. This did not seem to be due to the author's unwillingness or inability to contribute to the conversation – she had after all written the book. Moreover, I knew her to be a very intelligent and articulate person. I also noticed that she was interrupted in mid-sentence at least twice, although she did not interrupt anyone herself. Finally, although she was in her thirties and had completed a PhD, she was addressed by her first name by the host and other interviewers alike, and even at one point as 'my dear', unlike the others, who were always addressed by their formal academic titles.

The issues raised by this episode are complex. Initially, it was the topic of the book that had caught my attention, since it articulated an extreme position with respect to the role of language in relations between the sexes. What had captivated me, however, was the behaviour of the participants, enacting, in microcosm, the stereotype of male–female interaction.

Most people probably expect women and men to respond differently in similar situations, and as we shall see these expectations are not unreasonable in some cases, although in others they have no foundation in reality. On the other hand, knowledge of a person's sex is just one of many bases for everyday predictions of behaviour, as the above episode illustrates. I was expecting the author to respond in an assertive manner – even though she was female, and assertiveness is not typically associated with femininity. Now I needed to explain why her behaviour was at odds with my expectations. Were the interviewers responsible for her silence, bashing her into submission with an onslaught of assertiveness? Was she, after all, stereotypically feminine in her interaction style? Did the normative demands of the formal setting overwhelm the participants' individual dispositions? Was one of the interviewers going to be her PhD examiner? It even crossed my mind that the author had adopted a deliberate strategy in order to provide a subtle, living example of some of the things that she had written about.

I still do not know the answer, but the mere fact that I had been surprised by this apparently innocuous episode, and felt that it required explanation, indicated to me that I had come a long way in my thinking about language and the sexes. I was aware of the widely held social stereotypes as to what constitutes masculinity and femininity, and could articulate these in terms of concrete aspects of social conduct – speech style and interaction, in this case. Yet I did not fall back on these stereotypes to inform my predictions about an individual's behaviour: these were calibrated on the basis of my knowledge of the author as an individual and a social activist. Furthermore, when my expectations were disconfirmed, I sought information about the situation and the other participants, as well as the main target of my attention, in trying to formulate a satisfactory, if elusive, explanation. Finally, I was irritated by the behaviour of the interviewers, who I felt had treated the author in a patronizing and condescending manner, while at the same time depriving me of an opportunity to hear *her* speak, and I wondered if things could not have been different.

The themes that emerge in the discussion of this vignette are central to the whole area of language and sex research: sex differences, beliefs about sex differences and their impact on speech and communication; the influence of situations and individual differences; and attitudes, values and the need for social change. Each of these issues has been the focus of considerable research and comment in the past 15-20 years, as the ever-growing women's movement has sought to discover all the facts and forms of female–male differentiation in society. These aims coalesced with the goals of linguists, sociologists, anthropologists and psychologists, who at about the same time were busily engaged in studying the social aspects of language – social influences on language use, and the consequences of socially conditioned language patterns for communication, social evaluation and social change. The confluence of these two streams of activity produced a surge of publications defining the new and vital area of research on language and the sexes. We begin with a survey of the motives that have inspired most of this activity.

The Linguistic Impetus

There is no one key to understanding the tremendous growth of interest in this topic. However, pre-eminent among the stimuli to the growth and continuation of interests in language and the sexes has been the observation that men and women in most parts of the world speak somewhat differently on at least some occasions. Several examples of sex differences in speech had already been noted prior to 1900. The most famous of these concerns the Carib language of the Lesser Antilles, where at one time it was thought that women and men spoke distinct languages. Closer examination revealed that this was not the case, although there were extensive (by our standards) differences between the vocabularies of women and men, amounting to as many as one-tenth of the words spoken, and some differences in grammar

(Jespersen, 1922). The modern explanation for these phenomena centres on the fact that 'the Island Caribs are descended from Carib-speaking males and Arawak-speaking females whose males were slaughtered by the Caribs' (Hudson, 1980: 121). This historical fact cannot in itself explain the enduring differentiation between the sexes, however, and its perpetuation seems to have been due in part to superstitions regarding the pronunciation of some words by one sex or the other, and in part to the fact that the activities of traditional Carib society were highly differentiated along male–female lines (Jespersen, 1922; Taylor, 1951).

Similar observations were recorded intermittently by grammarians and dialectologists during the first half of the present century. Bodine (1975), in an excellent review, summarizes many of these findings, considering first differences in pronunciation and then differences in form. She enumerates three general types of pronunciation differences and three types of form, into which most of the existing data can be categorized. The first type of pronunciation difference is that where members of one sex group omit one or more sounds realized by the other sex. For example, Bogoras (1922) reported that male speakers of Chukchi, a Siberian language, often dropped consonants such as /n/ and /t/ when they occurred between vowels; and in some native American Muskogean languages (Haas, 1944), men often add a final /s/ to words.

Bodine's second and third types of pronunciation difference can be combined into one, thus yielding a category characterized by differences in either (1) the manner of articulation, or (2) the articulatory position of one or more speech sounds, with the number of sounds remaining the same for women and men. Two examples cited by Bodine and Bengali, where men often pronounce initial /n/ as /l/, and the American Indian Gros Ventre language, where women pronounce the male /tc/, /dj/ and /ty/ as /k/ and /ky/. Numerous examples from English language studies will be described later.

Differences in grammatical form have not been found frequently. The first of Bodine's three types is that where one sex-based version omits an affix used by the other sex. Bodine cites the native Californian language, Yana, as an instance: here, women dropped the final vowel of several forms. Another example is Japanese (Jorden, 1974), where the appearance of the sentence-final particle *ne* typically indicates a female speaker. The second type of form difference corresponds to the occurrence of different, though analogously patterned, affixes in women's and men's speech. In Thai, for example, women tend to emphasize the action of the verb by re-duplicating it (an appropriate example in English might be, *he beat and beat the rug until it was clean*), while men usually place a descriptive verb, *mak*, after the verb instead (Warotamasikkhadit, 1967). In the Dravidian language of Kŭṛux, only women pronounce the conjugation of verbs for the feminine gender, and then only when speaking with other women (Ekka, 1972). In several European languages, adjectives and descriptive nouns take affixes so as to agree in gender with the subject of the sentence. When the subject is also the speaker, this acts as a clue to the sex of the speaker (e.g., the sentence, *I am an actress* would be considered incorrect if spoken by a man).

The final grammatical form difference category suggested by Bodine is that where between one and several dozen words used by one sex have a different stem from those used by the other sex, but the other words are treated the same syntactically. The Carib example described above is probably the best of these. Several languages also have different pronouns, depending upon the sex of the speaker. Faust (cited, in Key, 1975) discusses this occurrence among the speakers of Cocama in South America. In Japanese the self-referents *Wasi* or *ore* indicate a male speaker, and in informal conversation, the occurrence of *watasi* or *atasi* are clues that the speaker is a woman (Jorden, 1974).

Differences in vocabulary have been frequently noted. Flannery (cited in Cappell, 1966) reports that women and men of the native North American Gros Ventre tribe used different interjections in discourse, and cites findings of similar phenomena among the Chaco of Paraguay and the Cuña of Panama. Jespersen (1922) discusses the case of Zulu women, for whom there is a taboo against uttering the names of their fathers-in-law, and even words that sound similar.

Frequently these early observations were accompanied by some perfunctory conjectures about the social significance or meaning of these differences. Such speculations notwithstanding, these studies were not concerned with describing or explaining the social order in general, or relations between the sexes in particular: rather, the goal was to contribute to our understanding of patterns of language use in society. This aim was accomplished chiefly by describing, in terms that appear crude and imprecise by today's standards, the relation between specified linguistic variables (using the terminology of the experimental method, the dependent variables or things to be explained) and other variables, both linguistic and non-linguistic (the independent variables, or tools of explanation), with which they had been observed to correlate, or in terms of which they could be predicted.

The emergence of sociolinguistics

By the 1960s, the vigorous activities of social scientists devoted to the study of language and society had earned for them the status of a new discipline, *sociolinguistics*. This rubric, however, encompasses a continuum of approaches to language and society, ranging from those whose aims are almost purely linguistic to those whose aims are entirely social (Trudgill, 1978). At the social scientific end, the aim is to study social knowledge and social pressures through talk, 'to use the linguistic data to get at the social knowledge that lies behind it, not to further our understanding about language' (Trudgill, 1978:4). At this end of the continuum, perhaps typified by ethnomethodology, inferences about society are based on assumptions about language behaviour. In the terminology used above, language behaviour assumes the role of the independent variable. At the linguistic pole of the continuum, assumptions are made about the society in order to shed light on linguistic phenomena. Thus, in the work of sociolinguists such as Labov and Trudgill, sometimes called 'secular linguistics', social phenomena (e.g. race, social class, sex, situation) are the independent variables in terms of which linguistic variation and change are interpreted; that is, phonological, syntactical and lexical features assume the role of the dependent variables. In fact, this is only part of the story, since an equally important facet of secular linguistics is the study of linguistic constraints on language phenomena. However, here we are concerned with the role of social constraints in so far as they can be considered independently of linguistic ones. Between the two poles of Trudgill's continuum can roughly be ordered applied sociolinguistics, the social psychology of language attitudes and bilingualism, and sociology of language, anthropological linguistics, the ethnography of speaking and discourse analysis, in terms of the relative contributions they make to the understanding of society, and linguistics, respectively (Smith, Giles and Hewstone, 1980).

Influences from the linguistic pole of Trudgill's continuum, where the aim is to account for the patterns of language variation and change, continue to exert a great impact on the shape of contemporary sociolinguistics (e.g., Chambers and Trudgill, 1980; Hudson, 1980; Romaine, 1982). This aim entails an active search for the parameters, both linguistic and non-linguistic, that most parsimoniously account for the distribution of the linguistic variables under scrutiny. The problem is, where to start searching? Confining our discussion to the search for non-linguistic, or social, correlates of speech variation, obvious candidates are those aspects of society that appear to lend it a structure or continuity that transcends the minutiae of individual differences and short-term fluctuations in social arrangements: large-scale, easily observable and relatively stable features such as race, ethnicity, nationality, socioeconomic status and, of course, sex. The observation that women and men speak differently qualifies sex for inclusion as an independent variable in the quest for descriptive linguistic parsimony.

The consolidation of secular linguistics

The consolidation of the linguistic impetus in modern sociolinguistics can be traced to the very rapid growth of methodological sophistication in studies of linguistic variation during the early 1960s. Labov's now classic study of the pronunciation of English in New York City (Labov, 1966) is often taken as a point of departure in this area.

Labov tape-recorded detailed interviews with 81 men and 117 women, and studied the distribution of five phonological variables among the speakers, who were chosen to be representative of the population of New York's Lower East Side. The independent social variables in terms of which phonological variation were analysed were: socioeconomic status (SES); ethnicity; sex; age; and social context, which was varied during the course of each interview from informal to formal. Labov was able to show that much of the linguistic variation, both between speakers and from one social context to another for any individual speaker, was the function of complex interactions among the four independent speaker characteristics. While SES appears to have been the speaker variable most predictive of linguistic variation in this study, sex, age and ethnicity also predicted some consistent patterns.

This research design represents the synthesis of several earlier methodological trends in sociolinguistics research, which, taken together, provided a model that is still influential today, especially for studies involving speaker sex. The most significant aspects of this model for present purposes are: (1) the choice of a non-exotic urban population; (2) the premeditated sampling of the population on the basis of several social parameters (age, sex, SES) simultaneously; (3) the observation of each informant in several different speech situations (in this case ranging from formal to informal), over which some degree of control was exerted to ensure uniformity or standardization of the procedure; (4) premeditated, precise measurement of several dependent phonological variables simultaneously; and (5) the wedding of linguistic, sociological and situational independent variables in a single research design.

Labov's masterful synthesis had an immediate impact on the status of sex as a variable in sociolinguistics. Whereas prior to the 1960s the observation of sex differences had been somewhat haphazard and casual, now it became almost *de rigueur* to include sex, usually just one among several large-scale social variables, in the systematic, quantitative study of variation. Furthermore, the advent of urban sociolinguistics resulted in a large corpus of new data on sex differences in modern, mostly English-speaking, societies. Finally, the combination of sex with other social variables, across a variety of speech situations, led to comparatively sophisticated views about sex as a factor in sociolinguistic variation (Smith, 1979).

On the basis of studies like these, several more of which will be described in chapter 5, a number of important descriptive conclusions were drawn about language and sex. The first thing to be noted is that sex differences are subtle and few; indeed, differences have sometimes not been found where they were expected (Labov, 1966; Fasold, 1972).

The second point is that almost all of the examples we have cited are instances of *sex-preferential* tendencies rather than *sex-exclusive,* all-or-none differences (Bodine, 1975). It is doubtful whether any examples of isolated sex-exclusive features could be found today. In most of the early studies, where we might be led to believe that they had been found, the authors were probably not sensitive to the distinction between sex-exclusive and sex-preferential speech. This distinction is an important one, for only if the correlation between a speech feature and sex is perfect is the inferential link between speech and sex a direct one. Otherwise, the observed covariation may be the result of a coincidental correlation of sex with another social division (e.g. occupation) which has stronger implications for speech than does sex. The authors of more recent urban linguistic surveys have pointed out that the speech variables they were interested in were usually better predicted by ethnicity, age and SES than by sex.

The third point, then, is that differences between female and male speech are not necessarily primarily markers of sex. The fourth point follows directly from the second and third and concerns a distinction between what I have called saturated and unsaturated usage (Smith, 1979). Even though some features and/or forms may be used by members of only one sex, they may be used by only some members. Taking a simplistic example, passionate monologues on the technicalities of football may be delivered only by men, but then only by *some* men. Thus, an apparently sex-exclusive feature may be an indicator not of sex as such, but rather of something that is itself a consequence of sex (in our example, sex-preferential interest in football), but does not saturate the sex group or cross the sex boundary.

Bearing these distinctions in mind, we can depict an idealized scheme within which the use of any speech feature, or features in combination, could be located in terms of both the proportion of members in each sex who use it, and the relative proportion of women and men who use it. In figure 1.1, points A and C represent sex-exclusive, saturated usage (possible examples are the different pronoun series used by women and men in Cocama and the male–female forms in Kŭṛux, both mentioned above). A feature that can be placed anywhere else in the scheme, except on the diagonal B, D (which represents equal usage by women and men), is technically an example of sex-preferential usage. Examples will be described at several points later in this book.

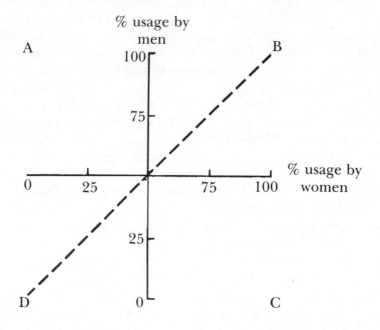

Figure 1.1   An idealized scheme for representing the relative use of a feature by women and men, and the proportion of members of each sex who use it

Finally, the position of a given speech feature in the scheme of figure 1.1 would almost certainly vary depending on the purpose of the interaction and the characteristics of the listener. To illustrate this, we need only consider languages in which the use of some forms depends on the sex of the listener, such as in Kŭṛux. Bodine (1975) gives several other examples where the sex of the listener influences the men's as well as the women's forms.

The Functional Impetus

Research on language and the sexes would not have gained the popularity it enjoys today if it had not been for the fact that recipes for the description of linguistic variation are enhanced by the inclusion of sex as an ingredient. However, the linguistic impetus has not, in and of itself, contributed much to our understanding of male–female relations. In fact, a stern appraisal would conclude that it has encouraged the opportunistic and uncritical exploitation of the sex variable as a static element of social structure, an unrefined explicator, rather than something to be itself explored and explained.

Secular linguistic extremists might protest that this is unfair, that it is not incumbent upon the sociolinguist, whose goals are linguistic, to be sociologically sophisticated: sex is just one of many first-order variables that will eventually be demonstrated to account more fully for sociolinguistic variation. In response, one must ask how, in a world of linguistic priorities, such first-order social variables are chosen. This is not easy to ascertain, for there is usually no explicit rationale given for these choices. It is clear, however, that they are not arbitrary. On the contrary, they are highly constrained, on the one hand by implicit theories about meaningful divisions in society, and on the other by intuitions about the potential for correlations between these divisions and the language variables under examination.

Thus, the exploitation of sex, age and SES as independent social parameters is not haphazard, but is based on shared intuitions about sources of variation in society. This illustrates simply that the choice of social variables is *not* governed entirely – perhaps not even primarily, in many cases – by the goal of descriptive linguistic parsimony. Instead, it is a result of a compromise between this goal and the unacknowledged desire to articulate discoveries about language in terms of meaningful social variables.

Sex is a convenient, very meaningful and highly salient variable in daily life. Yet there are dozens of human features that can provide the basis for equally exhaustive and apparently clear-cut divisions. Indeed, many of these are correlated with sex: height, weight, even shoe size. But these are not popular variables in sociolinguistics. Why? Because they are not seen to be as central to the dynamics of society, not as culturally meaningful as sex. The result: an uncritical, even complacent, reliance on the concept of sex as a simple categorical variable, with few attempts to explore the manner in which the concept is understood and deployed by people in society, in the construction of female–male relations.

In spite of this, we have seen that the research generated in the tradition described above has provided some useful starting points for our enquiry. It is to be hoped that the concern for social meaning, implicit and uncritical though it is, will not be sacrificed to the ends of descriptive linguistics in variation studies, which would thereby be relegated to the realm of purely academic exercises, bereft of social scientific relevance and practical importance.

Fortunately, the risk of this happening is small as long as the motives of sociolinguistics remain mixed, as they have so far. It is rarely in science that individual researchers can be identified uniquely with one and only one research motive. Indeed, the word 'impetus' has been chosen deliberately to describe the linguistic influence on contemporary sociolinguistics to avoid the implication that the contributions of researchers mentioned above can be relegated to the domain of descriptive linguistics.

In fact, almost all of the researchers mentioned above have offered some hypotheses as to the social meaning or significance of the differences they have observed, as did the earlier dialectologists. This is one of several different lines of thought and activity that betray a concern that is at the heart of the second major influence on language and sex research: that of illuminating the *social functions* of language in male–female relations.

The representation of women and men in language

One important line of activity stimulated by the functionalist impetus is concerned with how men and women are represented in language. Several aspects of contemporary English usage seem to reveal prejudicial attitudes demeaning and degrading women while glorifying men, thus apparently reflecting dominant social values. Conventions regarding forms of address, titles, word order and the use of pronouns, among other things, have been cited as evidence of a pro-male, or *androcentric*, bias in society (e.g. Nilsen *et al.*, 1977). Direct evidence from the study of dictionaries, textbooks, magazines and directly elicited sex stereotypes can also be brought to bear on the study of language and the representation of the sexes. These issues will be taken up in chapter 3.

There is more to this domain of activity than the interest in language as a social telltale, however. This is the concern that language, as the major vehicle for the transmission of beliefs and values of society, may profoundly *affect* female-male relations (e.g. Spender, 1980). One implication of this argument is that the attitudes transmitted help to reinforce the status quo – the subjugation of women and the dominance of men. By the same token, however, changes in language (e.g. the planned eradication of androcentric practices) would be expected to encourage changes in the status quo. These arguments are introduced in chapter 3, and discussed in greater depth in chapter 8.

The social significance of sex differences

Another important line of activity that can be subsumed under the functional rubric is concerned with the social meaning of sex differences in speech. Here, speculation abounds. Consider, for example, the conclusions of Danish linguist Otto Jespersen, who devoted a chapter of his influential book, *Language: Its Nature, Development and Origins* (1922), to the topic, 'The Woman'. Commenting on sex differences in word choice, he is confident that 'women exercise a great and universal influence on linguistic development through their instinctive shrinking from coarse and gross expressions and their preference for refined and (in certain spheres) veiled and indirect expressions' (p. 246). Men, on the other hand, are wary of the language becoming insipid at the hands of women; and, in striving to avoid the banal, 'men thus become the chief renovators of language'. He further notes that women as a rule have less extensive vocabularies than men, and that the science of linguistics can count among its votaries very few women. Men also, he concludes, have more intricate and involuted sentence structures than do women: 'Or we may use the simile that a male period is often like a set of Chinese boxes, one within another, while a feminine period is like a set of pearls joined together on a string of *ands* and similar words' (p. 252). Jespersen allows that these differences can be traced in part to differences in the socialization, education and division of labour between the sexes. But in the final analysis, he concludes that these are behavioural manifestations of evolutionary, biological trends; he invokes the concepts of 'instinct' (p. 256), 'human secondary sexual characters' (p. 248) and 'zoological facts' (p. 258), and refers frequently to the writings of Havelock Ellis.

Jespersen's observations are noteworthy primarily because they are among the best examples of early functionalist speculation. Leaving aside for the moment the debate about the validity of his remarks, we should note that Jespersen's conclusions pertain to the general hypothesis that sex differences in language use reflect or mark other sorts of differences between women and men. This is probably the most common type of functionalist hypothesis, and it will emerge again several times throughout the book. Too often in the past, however, contributions along these lines have remained at the level of loose speculation, with the consequence that fancy and stereotype sometimes have been misrepresented as fact (see chapters 4–7).

For the researcher who is seriously interested in this aspect of the functionalist pursuit, a triad of tasks awaits in the attempt to sketch the relations among a sociolinguistic phenomenon, its consequence and perhaps eventually its antecedents. The first task is to establish quantitatively the validity of the assertion that language differences exist where they are thought to exist.

Informal and intuitive claims have often proved difficult to substantiate. Neither is intuition sufficient when it comes to the task of discovering the social connotations of language variables, and the consequences of their use. Several reliable techniques exist for obtaining the evaluations and impressions from the population under investigation, who are, after all, the best arbiters of social meaning in their society (see chapter 4).

The third and most difficult task is to determine the antecedents of observed differences. As we have already noted, very few if any sex differences in speech are found to be perfectly correlated with the sex of the speaker. They are a matter of degree, and usually are sensitive to variations in context or situation. Such facts present the analytically minded with the problem of ruling out alternative hypotheses for the observations in an attempt to establish satisfactory causal explanations.

The management of interaction

The final domain in which the functionalist attitude prevails is in the study of conversation and interaction between the sexes, which is the topic of chapter 7. The predominant theme to have emerged from research of this type is that patterns of between-sex interaction mirror and reinforce social inequalities evident in other facets of female–male relations. In chapter 7 we will examine the ways in which communicative resources are put to work in the management of interaction and what they reveal about the sexes.

Beyond Functionalism: The Sociogenetic Impetus

While the linguistic impetus has provided some useful starting points for the study of language and relations between the sexes in the form of methodological tools and linguistic descriptions, the functional impetus has made great strides in the search for explanations of observed sex differences, and in broadening the scope of the enquiry to include the representation of men and women in language, the regulation of interaction, and the dynamics of social change. Yet, despite the variety of these contributions, and the dynamic, comprehensive analysis of female–male relations that they inspire, all of the research trends described so far start from the same basic point as regards their implicit assumptions about the nature of the groups, men and women. Most people take it for granted, without having to devote much time or thought to the matter, that there are two sexes, discrete and non-overlapping, defined by biological variables. We think of women and men as categories of nature, fundamentally distinct in at least some respects in spite of endless individual variation. In fact, a stronger form of this belief is probably more prevalent in our society: women and men, as groups, are seen to stand in binary opposition to each other. Whosoever is not one must be the other, a matter not of degree but of kind.

I believe that social scientists have not sufficiently studied the structure, origins and consequences of these assumptions. As a result, some important issues have been overlooked or ignored. In particular, very little attention has been directed to the problem of how the basic and pervasive distinction between men and women in our society is recognized and maintained: that is, how, in everyday life, are boys and men distinguished from girls and women? The question may seem trivial and the answers obvious at first blush, but I hope to convince you in the next chapter that they are not.

I will also argue that our thinking about men and women has led to a myopic concentration of research on sex differences, and that we need to understand more about how the sexes are maintained as distinct social categories before we can understand how and why they are different. Finally, I will suggest that too much emphasis has been placed on the uniformities of female–male relations, and not enough on the variable consequences of being a man or woman.

These points, their consequences for language and sex research and a framework that allows us to deal with them, are elaborated in chapter 2.

2

The Sociogenesis of Relations between the Sexes

The way in which we think about sex is typical of the way in which we respond as human beings to the challenge of an enormously complex environment: psychologically, we reduce complexity to manageable proportions. In particular, we seem to have a proclivity for organizing our knowledge of the environment not in terms of the continuity and flux that objectively characterizes a stimulus array, but in terms of discrete classes or categories of stimuli.

For example, although we can discriminate between an enormous number of different hues of colour, people the world over seem to organize the perception of and memory for colour around just 11 so-called 'focal' colours (Berlin and Kay, 1969). These are hues that people consistently pick out as being the 'best' exemplars of different colour categories in their language (Rosch, 1977).

It has been suggested that the psychological structure of colour categories, especially the high degree of cross-cultural consistency in the choice of focal colours, may in part reflect elementary constraints on visual perception imposed by the physiology of the human nervous system (Bornstein, 1975; Witkowski and Brown, 1977). Given the similarities in general nervous system structure associated with common species membership, it would be surprising not to find some – even many – instances where not only the predisposition to categorize, but also the form of the resultant categories, was cross-culturally similar. However, it is probably more generally true that the structure of psychological categories is variable: subject to modification through experience, sensitive to variations in the physical and social environments.

Most North Americans, for example, are not sensitive to regional and social variations in English as it is spoken in the British Isles, except perhaps to the point of being able to distinguish a Scottish or an Irish accent from an English one. To someone living in England, however, the differences between the accents typical of the working-class districts of London, Bristol, Birmingham, Liverpool and Newcastle, or between the counties of Dorset, Yorkshire and Sussex, are highly diagnostic, the objects of stereotype and even prejudice (see Giles and Powesland, 1975; Trudgill, 1978). Furthermore, these distinctions can be acquired relatively easily by North Americans who spend any length of time in England. The same is true of British subjects who spend time in North America – eventually they may come to recognize distinctions between the speech of people from the Deep South, New England and the Midwest, for example, and possibly even the subtle differences between cities or towns within the same region. It will not be difficult for you to think of many other examples of the plasticity of human categorization: in general, human knowledge and behaviour are highly susceptible to modification through experience, and the extent of this capacity for learning is undoubtedly one of the distinguishing features of our species.

Humans are also distinctive in the extent and complexity of the activities that they devote to influencing each other, both through direct instrumental manipulation and through the use of language and communication. Indeed, human societies are predicated upon the evolution and management of shared systems of knowledge and activity, tasks that demand extraordinary expenditures of effort (e.g. schooling, science, politics). Inevitably, much of this effort is devoted to the maintenance of shared systems of classification – of objects (e.g. foods, materials, tools), events (e.g. situations, episodes, predicaments) and people. We continually learn about and respond to people in terms of the categories and groups to which they belong. Sex, race, age, religion and occupation are only a few of the more salient large-scale dimensions of social categorization chosen from the repertoire of dimensions that we employ on a regular basis.

The ubiquitous proclivity for categorization is at once both a boon and a liability for the conduct of human affairs. On the one hand, by reducing the number and/or complexity of the dimensions in the perceived environment, it enables us to function effectively within the constraints of a remarkable, yet undeniably imperfect, nervous system. The simplification that results from the reduction of a continuous stimulus dimension to a few discrete values that subsume whole ranges along the continuum permits us, in a wide variety of situations, to ignore trivial variations within categories, and yet remain sensitive to important differences between them.

We must assume that, most of the time, category boundaries emerge in response to environmental variations that are compatible with material and social wellbeing. Knowledge of the social categories to which a person belongs is often of great help to us in forming impressions and making predictions about their attitudes and behaviour. Ultimately, we select our own strategies of interaction, in part to accommodate these predictions (Billig, 1976; Tajfel, 1981; 1982; Turner and Giles, 1981).

On the other hand, we pay for our propensity to categorize. Once categorized, entities tend to be judged and evaluated on the basis of their category membership, to the neglect of their individual attributes. Sensitivity to differences among individuals with categories may be reduced, while sensitivity to differences between categories is accentuated (Tajfel, 1981; Turner, 1981).

The Hypostatization of Sex

These effects of explicit categorization in the laboratory have their counterparts on a grander scale. Social science research and general public interest in the area of male–female relations reflects an overwhelming preoccupation with the uniformities of these relations. This is precisely what one would expect, given that the categories are in this context the focus of attention. Thus, social scientists have shown that women and men are represented differently in language (McConnell-Ginet, Borker, and Furman, 1980; Nilsen et al., 1977), do different work for different rewards (Equal Opportunities Commission, 1979; Hakim, 1979; International Labour Office, 1976), have access to different educational and career opportunities (Coussins, 1976), and are treated differently before the law (Land, 1978; Sachs and Wilson, 1978). Knowledge of a stimulus person's sex can influence judgements of their physical and mental health (Broverman *et al.*, 1970), products and performances (Deaux and Emswiller, 1974; Feather and Simon, 1973; Friend, Kalin and Giles, 1979; Ward, 1979), personality (Broverman *et al.*, 1972; Cicone and Ruble, 1978; Wlliams *et al.*, 1977), emotional experiences (Condry and Condry, 1976), and so on.

A more or less exclusive focus on the social consequences of being a man or a woman was an entirely justifiable and perhaps even necessary starting point for the study of male–female relations. However, this emphasis has led to a neglect of the consequences of variations in the degree to which people are seen as typical members of their sex. Research along these lines (see chapters 5 and 6) shows that these variations have a substantial impact on how people are treated, and on how they see themselves, thus urgently requiring that we develop a research sensitivity to the variable consequences of categorization and subsequent processes.

Another, perhaps even more significant, consequence of categorical thinking about men and women on the grand scale stems from the fact that, while the products of our categorizing activity are discernible and available to conscious reflection, the processes and mechanisms of categorization themselves usually are not. This leads to a process that I will term *psychological hypostatization*, whereby the categories in the eye of the beholder are endowed with an independent ontological status, an apparent intrinsic reality, apart from the processes that lead to their emergence and recognition in society. Consequently, the sexes are understood by most people as an inherent and/or God-given attribute of individuality, an inalienable, incontrovertible fact of human existence. Indeed, so ancient and well-groomed are these assumptions in our civilization that they seem almost to be true by definition and therefore unremarkable. Our belief in the independent 'reality' of sexual dimorphism has, psychologically speaking, assumed the proportions of an axiom of the human condition.

As a consequence, the categories female and male, appearing

self-evident, seem to require description rather than explanation. This tendency conspires with the above-mentioned emphasis on uniformity to create a climate in which it seems reasonable to assume that beliefs about the sexes and societal differences between them exist simply to accommodate intrinsic male–female differences. The outcome? A fantastic preoccupation among social scientists with the discovery and description of sex differences, the characteristics of the targets of social differentiation, and a relative poverty of attention devoted to the origins, development and significance of these categories in the lives of individuals (Deaux, 1984).

The existence of women and men as groups, and the prominence of sex as a focal point of social discrimination, requires at minimum the recognition and implementation of this distinction by individuals in society. This in turn requires a fuller appreciation of the mechanisms and dynamics of social categorization as perhaps the most basic link between the individual, as male or female, and society.

The Sexual Subculture

Sadly, we know little of a definite nature about how this categorization is achieved and maintained. Most would agree, however, that it is the appearance of the genitals at birth that provides the basis for what is probably the first, the most pervasive and the most stable organization of human beings into groups (Goffman, 1977; Kessler and McKenna, 1978). The categories originate for individuals in our society with their classification into one of two sex classes, male or female (Goffman, 1977). The conventional wisdom, of course, is that the categorization 'problem' posed to medical professionals and parents at the birth of a newborn is a trivial one, and that the vast majority of neonates can instantly be recognized as well-formed males or females. Be this as it may, and the truth of this wisdom has yet to be tested, the first step in the process of initiation into a sex class is an act of categorization, which reduces the significant variations in genital appearance that are characteristic even of newborns to a simple binary classification.

This initial classification is undoubtedly one of the most important things that ever happens to us. To society, a baby's sex is second in importance only to its health; more important than colouration in ethnically homogeneous, and perhaps even in ethnically diverse, societies; more important than size or temperament. From the moment of birth, genital anatomy is a cue for all sorts of discriminative beliefs, expectations and behaviours. Yet the dynamics of male–female relations and the eventual ramifications of sex classification are scarcely betrayed by the elegance of its original induction:

> Every society seems to develop its own conception of what is 'essential' to, and characteristic of, the two sex classes, this conception embracing both praised and dispraised attributes. Here are the ideals of masculinity and femininity, understandings about ultimate human nature which provide grounds (at least in Western society) for identifying the whole of the person, and provide also a source of accounts that can be drawn on in a million ways to excuse, justify, explain, or disapprove the behaviour of an individual or the arrangement under which he [sic] lives, these accounts being given both by the individual who was accounted for and by such others as have found reason to account for him [sic]. Norms of masculinity and femininity also bear on the objective (albeit mainly socially acquired) differences between the sex-classes, but, as suggested, do not coincide with these differences, failing to cover some, misattributing others, and, of course, accounting for a considerable number by means of a questionable doctrine – in our society, a doctrine of biological influences.
>
> In so far as the individual builds up a sense of who and what he [sic] is by referring to his sex class and judging himself in terms of the ideals of masculinity (or femininity), one may speak of *gender identity*. It seems that this source of self-identification is one of the most profound our society provides, perhaps even more so than age-grade, and never is its disturbance or change to be anticipated as an easy matter. [Goffman, 1977: 303–4; italics in original]

Goffman's description of the sexual subculture is an extremely succinct and heuristic portrayal of the fundamental elements of male–female relations in our society or, as he calls it, the 'arrangement between the sexes'. However, there are several assumptions implicit in the concept of a sexual subculture that ought to be made explicit before we proceed.

First, the concept implies that there is a relatively coherent sphere of human thought and activity pertaining to sex and gender, distinct from (but possibly interacting with) thought and activity regarding other dimensions of social categorization (e.g. race, class, religion). Second, it is meaningful to speak of a sexual subculture only to the extent that the fundamental assumptions, perceptions and practices regarding sex and gender are similar from community to community within society. Finally, it suggests that all members of society share more or less equal responsibility for the form of the subculture. Each of these assumptions requires empirical attention before we can conclude that Goffman's characterization of male–female relations in terms of a sexual subculture is apt. However, the treatment of these topics in any detail is well beyond the scope of the present work, and I will continue to use the terms 'sexual subculture', 'gender' and 'gender identity' in much the same way throughout the rest of the book, subscribing to the notion of the sexual subculture as a kind of working hypothesis.

Cross-cultural Variation

In this society, and apparently in most others, the sexual subculture is characterized by a 'two and only two' structure, which not only forces practically everyone into one or the other sex category, but does not tolerate negative correlations between sexual anatomy and gender (Martin and Voorhies, 1975, chapter 4; Stoppard and Kalin, 1978). Furthermore, the convergent gender-characteristic attributes are highly correlated in the ideology of the subculture, so that anatomy, personal appearance, personality, sexual and much non-sexual behaviour form a tight cluster. The most deep-seated feature of this cluster appears to be anatomical sex. In short, the gender formulae are relatively cohesive, cross-situationally prominent and reciprocal, and hinge on a simple anatomical fact.

It is crucial to note that the features apparently typical of this sexual subculture are not necessarily characteristic of subcultures in other cultural contexts, which also appear to originate with and revolve around classification on the basis of genital appearance. Martin and Voorhies (1975) provide brief scenarios of several non-industrial settings, where more than two sex classes and/or gender formulae are in evidence. The Navajo, for example, appear to have recognized a separate sex class for individuals who were anatomically distinct from females and males, whom they call 'real nadle'. This third sex class corresponds to a gender formula for *nadle*, which may also be aspired to by anatomical males or females, i.e. 'those who pretend they are nadle'. In other words, 'real nadle' are not forced into the male or the female gender pattern as they would be in our society. Furthermore, the *nadle* gender formula constitutes a real third-gender option, and not just a misfit category, as evidenced by the possibility of men and women adopting *nadle* status. The Mohave, while apparently recognizing only two sex classes, allowed some females to adopt masculine-like statuses, called *hwame.*, and some males to adopt a feminine-like gender, called *alyha.*, status changes that are recognized in ceremonial initiations. There are several other examples that illustrate the variability of the relationship between sex class and gender, as well as the less cohesive nature of gender formulae in some cultures. Sex, rather than a self-evident fact of social organization, is in the first instance the result of consensus about the characteristics, physical, behavioural and otherwise, that distinguish men from women.

The hypothesis that genital sex is universally a basis for pervasive social discrimination appears to be well-founded, although the complexity of the resulting social arrangements and the implications for members of different categories vary enormously. It would certainly be wrong to assume, for example, that the point of insertion of this categorization into the complex network of intersecting categorizations that characterizes people's understanding of society is invariant from culture to culture, with respect to either its functional significance or its subjective prominence. This raises the possibility that our (Western, industrial) definition of the everyday criteria that distinguish the sexes, and our understanding of the nature of sex in society, is ethnocentric, and the meaning of sex differences and differentiation could not be assumed to be cross-culturally constant. This is seldom acknowledged in language and sex research, and findings from widely different cultural contexts are cited in support of hypotheses about 'male–female relations' in general. Although I will refer occasionally to cross-cultural data in this book, I do so primarily for the purposes of illustration and contrast. In the main, I will confine my comments to data gathered in the English-speaking world, and assume that there is a large degree of similarity among the sexual subcultures of these societies.

Beyond Categorization: Sex Stereotypes and Evaluations

The most elementary function of the sexual subculture is to ensure that people are equipped with concepts of masculinity and femininity that enable them to distinguish between women and men. It has to be able to accommodate a number of additional complexities, however. For example, the fact that we are accustomed to wearing clothing that conceals the pivotal cues to a person's sex rarely interferes with our readiness or ability to make a judgement. Nor by all accounts should it, since so-called secondary sex characteristics (body shape and size, presence or absence of facial hair, characteristics of the voice) correlate very highly with anatomical sex. Yet if the cultural reduction of genital variation to a two-way system is evidence of categorization, then our reliance upon these secondary characteristics, which are distributed among people in a much more obviously continuous way, is even more so. In other words, our ability to use these cues so efficiently attests to the scope and power of our shared conceptual framework. Of course, our task is made easier by fashion-related cosmetic and non-verbal cues, including names, that are carefully managed to accentuate the category boundary.

Nevertheless, it is evident that the pivotal role of anatomy as marker of sex is superseded, or at least reduced in importance, for most people for most of the time. The question remains as to exactly what cues are used in making inferences about a person's sex when the primary cues are not available. A medical professional might defer to physiological, hormonal or genetic cues, since they correlate so well with sex class, and might even be said to cause the appearance of the anatomical features to which we react (although *potentiate* might be a better term to describe the complex interaction among genetic material, hormones and anatomy: Hutt, 1972; Money and Ehrhardt, 1972). Or one might defer to functional reproductive criteria such as the capacity to menstruate, bear children and lactate, or to produce sperm and ejaculate. These functional criteria probably explain why genital anatomy is universally so important as a criterion for categorization: from a sociocultural point of view, genital anatomy is a predictor of reproductive potential, just as, from a biological point of view, hormonal and genetic factors predict the appearance of the reproductive organs. However, just as knowledge of biological information is insufficient to predict with certainty genital appearance and thereby sex class, so is knowledge of sex class insufficient to predict with certainty one's reproductive role.

Ultimately, then, anatomy is important in so far as it is a building block for social organization, and categorization is only the tip of an iceberg as far as the impact of the sexual subculture on the lives of individuals is concerned. The lines along which gender is expected to unfold, the stages it progresses through and the situational constraints to which it is subject are matters for empirical attention. It requires a systematic attempt to discover the convergent, and perhaps sometimes even competing, attributes, behaviours and so on that result in one being treated, and hopefully feeling, 'as a woman' or 'as a man' in a variety of situations.

Beliefs about sex differences are a very pervasive feature of our society and can be easily documented in literature for children, teenagers and adults (Kramarae, 1981), in television (Howitt, 1982), in educational resources (Gershuny, 1977; Nilsen, 1977b), and in commercial advertisements (Courtney and Whipple 1974; Goffman, 1976), to name but a few. These beliefs are usually called *sex stereotypes,* and they include, in addition to beliefs about very basic and quintessential differences such as those described in the preceding section, beliefs about important but non-essential differences (in personality and emotion, for example -- see chapter 3) and even trivial ones (for instance, beliefs about sex differences in colour vocabulary). Bruce Feirstein's (1982) satire of contemporary masculinity in North America, subtitled *A Guidebook to All That is Truly Masculine*, proclaims in its title: *Real Men Don't Eat Quiche*. The book includes sections on: 'The Real Man's Library' (e.g. Ian Fleming's *Goldfinger*); 'Real Men and Television' (sports, Westerns, police dramas); 'The Real Man's Nutritional Guide' (e.g. 'as a general rule, Real Men won't eat anything that is poached, sautéed, minced, blended, braised, curried, flambéd, stir-fried, or en brochette'); and 'Two Colours That Do Not Appear in a Real Man's Wardrobe' ('Puce. And mauve'). His lightheartedness notwithstanding, Feirstein has succeeded in capturing the gist and scope of some important (American) masculine values.

This kind of portrayal nicely illustrates another fact, namely that stereotypes rarely carry connotations of 'different but equal': people have definite and conspicuous attitudes about which sex is 'better' or 'superior' for any of the putative differences, and it has been a matter of some debate as to which sex is more positively valued in this sense (chapter 3).

Taken together, sex stereotypes and the attitudes held in respect of them constitute our social representations of men and women as distinctive social groups, the formulae for masculinity and femininity. An important and interesting domain of representation concerns the way men and women sound and use language. As we shall see in chapters 4, 6 and 7, extensive evidence indicates that we have stereotypes about vocal, intonational, paralinguistic, phonological, grammatical, vocabulary and stylistic differences between the sexes, many of which also carry clear evaluative connotations.

Social Judgement, Impression Formation and Gender Identity

So far I have considered primarily the ideological dimension of the sexual subculture, the shared constructs and representations of women and men as distinct categories within society. The discovery and description of stimuli that are among the bases for social discrimination (the speech correlates of perceived masculinity and femininity in this case) are worthwhile pursuits in themselves. Yet it must be borne in mind that social perception and attribution are situated, consequential activities, susceptible to the influence of interpretation, reaction and other factors that involve the targets of judgement. Let us turn, therefore, to consider the impact of the ideology of the sexual subculture on members of society.

As we have already seen, the social and material consequences of being born female or male are extremely varied and serious. This presumably reflects something of the richness of our gender formulae and their influence in society. On the other hand, it is easy to demonstrate that there is not a direct one-to-one correspondence between the ideology of the sexual subculture and relations between women and men, since: (1) sex stereotypes seriously misrepresent the nature and extent of sex differences at any particular time, and (2) men and women vary in their masculinity and femininity, which they would not do if they responded uniformly to the gender formulae (e.g. Nichols, 1962; Spence and Helmreich, 1978).

However, a direct correspondence is not necessary in order to demonstrate that our constructs of masculinity and femininity influence our reactions to men and women. Although research in this area is scanty, it would suggest that our preconceptions, rather than determining our reactions, shape and constrain them. Once we have satisfactorily categorized someone as male or female, our gender constructs come into play, providing us with judgemental standards against which to compare a person in forming impressions about their masculinity and femininity. The attributes and behaviours about which we have explicit sex stereotypes ought then to be important sources of information in this process of impression formation, and the research reviewed in chapters 4, 6 and 7 indicates that speech variables figure prominently among these.

As we shall see, though, the preoccupation with sex differences, and with the consequence of a person's sex alone for judgements made of that person, have hindered the development of a perspective that is sensitive to patterns of variation in the application and consequences of masculinity/femininity judgement, and the processes underlying these variations.

From among the great variety of factors that could conceivably underlie variations in the attribution of masculinity and femininity, two of the most important are chosen for examination in chapter 6. The first and perhaps most obvious concerns the degree to which attributions to people of masculinity and femininity correspond to their own masculine and feminine self-images. Despite the fact that most theorists explicitly posit some form of interplay between an individual's self-assessed masculinity and femininity and that attributed to them by others (e.g. Goffman, 1977; Kessler and McKenna, 1978; Parson, Frieze and Ruble, 1976), virtually nothing is known about the vehicles that serve this interaction, or about the form that it takes. More specifically, not one of the studies reviewed in chapter 4 involves an examination of how speech-based attributions of femininity and masculinity correspond to the speaker's self-assessed femininity and masculinity or *gender identity* (Goffman, 1977). The original empirical research reported in chapter 6 is addressed primarily to this remarkable lacuna, where it is shown that listeners form impressions of speakers' masculinity and femininity that are not only reliable, but also correspond closely to speakers' masculine and feminine self-images.

The second possible source of variation in masculinity/femininity attribution chosen for study here is concerned with characteristics of the judges rather than with those of the judged. Specifically, the consequences of variations in listeners' own masculinity and femininity for masculinity and femininity attributions to speakers will be examined. These two lines of enquiry will be augmented with two experiments to discover if judgements of masculinity and femininity are accompanied by systematic evaluative judgements.

Before these experiments are described, it is necessary to invervene with a description and critique of the methods that have been used to measure masculinity and femininity (chapter 5). There are at least eight standardized and apparently well-established instruments that purport to measure individual masculinity and femininity in various ways. It would seem to be a relatively straightforward matter to choose one of these as a means to discovering how speech-based attributions of femininity and masculinity are related to the speakers' own gender identities, and how they are influenced by listeners' masculinity and femininity. Such is not the case, however, as the short historical review of masculinity/femininity measurement in chapter 5 will show. Here it will be seen that two different methods of masculinity/femininity measurements have evolved (the *sex difference method* and the *self-categorization method*), only the latter of which is in principle compatible with the aims of the present research. The sex difference method, which relies upon sex differences in response to defining and measuring masculinity and femininity, has been faulted by numerous others on both theoretical and methodological grounds. This disillusionment foreshadowed a transition away from a sex difference criterion of masculinity and femininity, and towards a measurement technique based loosely on self-assessed conformity to sex stereotypes. The transition of the self-categorization method is not yet complete, however, and contemporary masculinity/femininity instruments fall short of fulfilling their theoretical promise in several important ways. Recommendations for revisions are made, and these are applied in the experiment described in chapter 6.

But, first, let us return to the task of discovering more about language and the social representation of men and women.

3

Language and the Representation of Women and Men

Language, in the form of popular, educational, artistic and scientific literature, informal conversation and formal rhetoric, conveyed at first hand or with the aid of intervening media, is the repository of our shared wisdom (or lack of it) about the sexes. It is also the main vehicle whereby this wisdom is disseminated throughout society, between generations and across cultures – to be interpreted and accepted, or challenged, debated, transformed and rejected, and ultimately put to work in constructing the fabric of the sexual subculture. Many aspects of social representation will be discussed in this chapter, ranging from the overt caricaturization of women and men in the media to the subtleties of the English lexicon, and from features of direct interaction to the innuendo that is implicit in indirect references to men and women. Taken together, they comprise a concert of small effects, whose significance far exceeds the sum of its individual parts. Furthermore, many people have sought to capture the essence of male–female distinctiveness, as it is represented in the beliefs of the sexual subculture, in terms of simple analogies and metaphors. These themes lend a great deal of structure to our thinking about women and men, and a few of the more important ones will be introduced in the final section.

Archival Data

Women and men in the media

A local newspaper story with the title 'Girl Talk' describes the final round of talks between English Prime Minister Thatcher and

Indian Prime Minister Ghandi in New Delhi. A headline in another newspaper reads, 'Barrister and Woman Found Dead'. An advertisement for the luxury liner Queen Elizabeth II proclaims, 'QE II "Wife Free" fares across the Atlantic. They add to the pleasure but not the price.' 'Drivers: Belt the wife and kids – and keep them safe', advises a road safety poster in London. An illustration of a pneumatic young woman in underwear and a suspender belt adorns an advertisement for an automobile paint and body shop that reads, 'you can't fault a good body'. A billboard ad for a Fiat car says, 'If it were a lady it would get its bottom pinched.' Underneath someone has written, 'If this lady was a car, she'd run you down.'

These and hundreds of other examples that have been culled from the pages of the British press, in 'The Naked Ape' column of the *Guardian* newspaper (Veitch, 1981; White and Wood, 1982), betray pervasive and systematic asymmetries in the portrayal of women and men in the mass media. Undoubtedly, many different kinds of asymmetries can be discovered, although knowledge in this area is as yet too meagre to permit a comprehensive taxonomy.

Most studies of the social representation of the sexes in the media have concentrated on aspects of content (Howitt, 1982). For example, Courtney and Whipple (1974) reviewed the results of four studies that analysed the roles of women in television commercials, all of which suggested very similar conclusions. Almost 90 per cent of the authority figures in these commercials, represented by the voice-over commentary of an announcer or a product representative, were males. As far as the occupational roles of the characters in the commercials, females were portayed much more often in domestic roles, while males dominated the media/celebrity, and sales/management occupational categories. Furthermore, even when women were portrayed in the role of product representative, they were more often seen performing domestic tasks involving the advertised product, while males were most often seen demonstrating novel features of the product. Finally, 'the female product representative tends to be a young housewife performing domestic duties within the home. The male product representative is older and tells her what to do and why' (p. 116). More recent studies (e.g. Maracek *et al.*, 1978) support major aspects of the earlier work, and show that not much change has taken place in the intervening years.

Magazine fiction has also been slow to respond to societal change. Despite large changes in the makeup of the US labour force since 1940 – the proportion of working women has increased by 60 per cent since then – no important changes in the relative number of male and female characters in magazine stories were detected over the same period (Lazer and Dier, 1978). Howitt (1982) reviews a variety of additional evidence pertaining to the depiction of women and men in children's television programmes, on women's daytime television serials and on prime-time television, all of which goes to suggest that the roles and images in terms of which the sexes are represented in the media conspire to create an image that is, not surprisingly, generally in line with widespread sex stereotypes.

Gender advertisements

Goffman's (1976) analysis of more than 500 pictorial advertisements depicting women, men and children leads him to the conclusion that 'Advertisers conventionalize our conventions, stylize what is already a stylization, make frivolous use of what is already something considerably cut off from the contextual controls. Their hype is hyper-ritualization' (p. 84). His analysis includes observations, all illustrated with representative advertisements, on the role of physical stature in portrayals of status and authority (characters with higher status, nearly always male, are bigger), the use of physical arrangements between people, of costumes and uniforms, and stereotypical body postures to convey relations of authority and deference, dominance and subordination in advertisements. 'In contrived scenes in advertisements, men tend to be located higher than women, thus allowing elevation to be exploited as a delineative resource' (p.43); 'women frequently, men very infrequently, are posed in a display of the "bashful knee-bend" ' (p.45); 'having somewhat the same distributions in ads as the knee-bend are canting postures... the resulting configurations can be read as an acceptance of subordination, an expression of ingratiation, submissiveness, and appeasement' (p. 46).

Dreams for teens

Kramarae (1981) reviews the representation of the sexes in publications aimed at the teenage market, many of which have circulations in the hundreds of thousands. 'Clearly,' she concludes, 'the interests of adolescent females and adolescent males are thought to be different.' Publications aimed at girls are classified in the *Standard Periodical Directory* (Garry, 1973) as 'romantic fiction touching upon some of the personal and social problems faced by today's teen', while male-oriented magazines are described as 'authentically written and drawn tales of the world of wheels', or 'shoot-em-ups and showdowns in the old romantic West', or 'set against combat-zone backgrounds from World War I to Vietnam'. Kramarae suggests that these topic differences correspond to differences in the way female and male adolescents are evaluated and are expected to behave.

What, then, do we make of all the asymmetries that have been described above? It is tempting to ask whether they help to create the very differences in society that they portray, or merely reflect differences that already exist. But to phrase the question in this way, in the form of a disjunction, suggests that only one of these two alternatives can be true, whereas, on the contrary, social representations of males and females in the media and elsewhere undoubtedly serve both functions, neither one perfectly.

Let us take first the function of social reflection, which concerns the agenda that informs the selection and creation of images by those who control the media. These people probably seldom see it as their role simply to reconstruct societal reality. Artistic considerations almost certainly intrude into these processes, as undoubtedly do commercial and political factors, especially in societies where the survival of most media resources is determined in the marketplace. From this perspective, we require systematic information about the sorts of factors that influence the decision-making processes of editors, producers and programme directors, including the relative impact of stereotypes about audience appeal, viewer ratings and tactics to keep commercial sponsors. This will help us to understand more about how and why media images deviate from social reality. A fact that cannot be ignored is that men continue to occupy the great majority of such influential decision-making positions in media-related industries.

Turning to the impact that these images have upon society, the major determining factor here is the attitude of the consumer, who is capable of being naive and gullible, sophisticated and cynical, and simply distracted and entertained, although perhaps not all at once. An audience's attitude towards the source of communication must be considered of the utmost importance in determining their reaction to a message. A communicator who lacks credibility and authority, who is dissimilar to the audience or untrustworthy, will tend not to be persuasive, and therefore will not stimulate role-modellling. (For a comprehensive review of the literature on persuasion, see Petty and Caccioppo, 1981.) Most of us take our media with a large pinch of salt and are thereby hopefully protected against mindless, uncritical subservience to media-perpetuated stereotypes. This is not intended as a lullaby into complacency, however. The fact is that we understand little of a definite nature about the trade in images between society and the media. Just because it is not a simple relation does not imply that a relation does not exist, and we must continue to research the two-way street between media portrayals and the social facts of female–male relations.

Reference Materials

Whatever one might think about the antecedents and consequences of social representation in the media, the less cynical among us would probably like to believe that things are somehow different when it comes to the construction of reference and educational materials, such as dictionaries, textbooks and school readers. Let us defer for a moment the discussion of how we might expect things to be different, and describe a few studies that have addressed the issue of social representation in these sources.

Graham (1975) describes the results of an analysis made of sentences taken from children's books and magazines that were used to illustrate word entries in the 1974 school edition of the

American Heritage Dictionary. Reference to boys and men far outnumbered references to girls and women. Use of the words *he, him* and *his* was almost four times more frequent than the use of *she, her* and *hers.* Of course, this discrepancy could have been due in part to the convention of using *he* in a generic sense as a shorthand for referring to people in general. To test this possibility, Graham obtained a random sample of 940 citation sentences containing *he* and found that only 3 per cent could be interpreted in the generic sense. Almost 80 per cent referred explicitly to a male human being, 14 per cent referred to male animals, and the remaining uses referred to agents like farmers and sailors, nouns with strong masculine connotations (see p. 45).

Other inferences were drawn from the sentences analysed: the depiction of men, boys and sons greatly outnumbered the depiction of women, girls and daughters; all firstborn children were boys; the role of parent, guardian or older relative was depicted much more often in relation to a male than to a female child. A similar analysis carried out on illustrative sentences in the 1966 Random House *Dictionary of the English Language* suggests that, quite apart from the relative prominence of male and female characters, they are portrayed in very different roles. Females are more frequently associated with domestic contexts (mothers, wives, hostesses, etc.), the world of fashion and glamour and in emotional situations. Males are most often portrayed in the roles of delinquent, rebel and bad guy (!) and in roles related to business and finance (Gershuny, 1977).

These are just a few of the more concrete and quantifiable sorts of asymmetries in texts and dictionaries that have been described. The authors cited above discuss numerous others, which result in images for women and men that are very similar to those gleaned from the mass media. Let us return now to consider how and why we might have considered things to be different.

First, consider the agenda of those who create and control these resources. While commercial considerations undoubtedly intrude on the writers and publishers of dictionaries and textbooks in much the same way as they do elsewhere, one would hope that the producers of such materials would be constrained by the criteria of objectivity and realism, at least at the level of constructing images that reflect the relative numbers of men and women in society, and the variety of the roles that they perform. Such is apparently not the case, and many writers have argued that creators of educational and reference materials must accept a large share of the responsibility for the perpetuation of unjust inequalities between women and men.

So far, I have not directly tackled the issue of what impact, if any, asymmetries in social representation have on society. This issue will be taken up later in this chapter, and throughout the rest of the book. For the moment, let me simply draw attention to some factors that may lead us to expect that asymmetries in these sources may be more consequential than media portrayals. First, students are less free to disregard or be critical of educational materials than they are of the media. In fact, they are frequently required to absorb and assimilate this material in minute detail. Second, people attach a great deal of credibility and authority to educational and reference material, and are therefore probably much more attentive to the messages that they convey, and susceptible to the sway of their influence.

Paradigmatic Woman and Man

Many other poignant observations have been made about archival representations of the sexes, a few of which will be described below. Some of these involve analyses of the English lexicon. Nilsen (1977a), for example, describes an analysis of 517 words chosen from a dictionary according to the semantic criterion that they possessed a clear and overt semantic marker of masculinity (e.g. man, son, fraternize) or femininity (e.g. woman, girl, actress). The words were also analysed according to the presence or absence of a number of other semantic criteria, such as prestige, and negative connotation. Predictably, masculine words outnumbered feminine words, by a ratio of 3:1. Masculine words denoting prestige (defined as either skill or power over others) were six times as frequent as feminine prestige words (examples include *alderman, craftsmanship, first lady, motherhood*). However, feminine words with negative connotations (e.g. *fishwife, callgirl, old maid*) outnumbered negative masculine words (*fallguy, hangman, madman*) by about 20 per cent, in spite of the predominance of masculine words overall! Nilsen also draws attention to the large number (at least 80) of overtly masculine words that are sometimes used in a generic sense, including *bachelor's degree, brotherhood, fellow man, mankind, master, spokesman* and *workmanlike.* Feminine generics do not occur (see p. 48).

There are certainly more rigorous approaches to semantic analysis than the one employed by Nilsen, but her description is nevertheless revealing. So too is Stanley's (1977a) compilation of 220 words with explicit sexual connotations that are applied to women: she documented only 22 for men.

Talking to Men and Women

Beginning with names

How many times a day do you identify yourself to someone by name? Try to keep a record sometime and you may find that it is much more often than you at first imagine – when introducing yourself to a stranger, talking on the telephone, signing a cheque, etc. Now think of how often you refer to other people by *their* names, either in their presence or in their absence. It will probably be many times more often than you refer to yourself.

The point of this exercise, which hardly needs so graphic an illustration, is that names are important. For most of us, a name is much more than just a tag or a label. It is a symbol which stands for the unique combination of characteristics and attributes that defines us as an individual. It is the closest thing that we have to a shorthand for the self-concept.

People the world over are named according to public and sometimes very formal social customs. Ryan (1981) describes naming practices among the Hausa of northern Nigeria; infants are first given a so-called 'secret' name, and only on the seventh day after birth is the infant taken outside its mother's hut and given its public name. Among the Muslim Hausa, this name-giving is accompanied by a formal ceremony, called 'Ranar Suna', that marks the passage of the child into Hausa culture. The majority of the names given at the naming ceremony are selected from the Koran. Hausa naming practices do not stop here, though, for the individual will later acquire nicknames bestowed by parents, grandparents, siblings, relatives or friends. They may also acquire 'phrase-names', which record important events concerning an individual's family. Ryan describes even more name categories that Hausa individuals may collect, from among which they choose the one or ones they prefer.

Among the Yoruba of south-western Nigeria, the bestowal of personal names proceeds according to a very different pattern (Akinnaso, 1981). While people go through a naming ceremony similar to that practised by the Hausa, among the Yoruba a person's name is chosen chiefly to satisfy the requirements of the proverb, 'The condition of the home determines a child's name.' In other words, the name is chosen to reflect culturally salient events or activities surrounding the child's home context at or about the time of birth.

The customs that apply throughout most of the Judeo-Christian world are well-known, even if only implicitly. Our names are usually comprised of two main parts: a so-called family name or surname, and at least one given name. Local, ethnic and religious traditions may sometimes prescribe certain patterns regarding the allocation of given names, as a means of preserving the memory of important figures. There is one convention, however, to which all others involving name-giving are subordinate, and this is that the name be chosen to reflect the child's sex.

The vast majority of given names in our society carry clear feminine or masculine connotations. Names like Dale and Lee, which are considered acceptable for both males and females, are rare. Familiar and apparently ambiguous names, like Jo, Chris and Pat, are usually abbreviations of longer unambiguous forms – such as Joseph or Joanne, Christine or Christopher, and Patricia or Patrick.

Given names, then, with which we usually become enduringly associated within a few days of birth, efficiently reinforce the male-female dichotomy within our society. The structure of given names may reveal more than this about relations between the sexes, however. It is possible, for example, that more male than female given names are passed directly from one generation to the next. I would predict this because: (1) greater value is placed on the achievements of males than on those of females, and men get more public recognition than women do; hence men's names have acquired more symbolic value; and (2) children typically inherit their father's rather than their mother's family name (see below, which enables fathers but not mothers to achieve a direct continuity of naming from generation to generation, provided they have sons. Even if there are only daughters, however, the derivation of female forms from male names (Collette, Georgina, Henrietta, Josephine, Paulette, Stephanie, Victoria) enables the transmission to continue.

Note that there are few if any female-to-male derivations in common use. Note further that a common method of deriving a female name from a masculine one is to add a diminutive suffix such as -ette, a practice that, it has been suggested, diminishes the strength of the name (Miller and Swift, 1976).

Miller and Swift also point out that there is a method whereby women can achieve at least some degree of continuity of names between generations. This is possible where custom permits a woman to bestow a family name from her side of the family upon one of her daughters as a given name. But this is a practice usually reserved for males. Miller and Swift note that family names such as Leslie, Beverley, Evelyn and Sidney may have lost their appeal as boys' given names because they were also handed on from mother to daughter in the same manner as described above. In any case, it is obvious that this method can be considered only partially successful for women, since in all probability the name that they are trying to preserve could eventually be traced to a male, not a female, ancestor, owing to our practices regarding the perpetuation of family names.

Family names

The assumptions that underlie the customs regarding family names in our society are even more revealing. Although by no means universal, it is still very common for women in Europe and North America to adopt their husband's family names when they marry. Thus, 'women are said to "marry into families"; and families are said to "die out" if an all-female generation occurs. The word family, which comes from the Latin *famulus*, meaning a servant or slave, is itself a reminder that wives and children, along with servants, were historically part of a man's property' (Miller and Swift, 1976:9). Considering the implications of this practice, Spender (1980:24) comments: 'Practically, it means that women's family names do not count and that there is one more device for making women invisible.'

Not only do naming conventions reflect and remind us of relations between the sexes in the past: they affect these relations now and in the future, argues Spender. She uses the phrase 'making women invisible' to capture the sense in which she believes that these and other language-related devices contribute to the subordination of women in society (see also Bate, 1975).

Miller and Swift's contention that women tend to be defined in relation to the men that they marry is also supported by our use of the titles *Miss, Mrs* and *Mr*. The contrastive pair, *Mrs/Miss*, is widely used to distinguish married from unmarried women, while a similar contrast is not applied to men. It is only since the early nineteenth century that these titles have served their present function in English; prior to that, *Mrs* was applied to all adult women, and *Miss* to female children. Miller and Swift suggest that the change in the use of these forms to denote marital status arose as a consequence of women's changing roles during the Industrial Revolution. To the extent that wage labour enabled more women to achieve an identity and means of existence independent of men, the use of the titles *Mrs* and *Miss* became popular as a means of communicating information about a woman's sexual availability. The implication is that marital status was an important component of women's – but not of men's – public social identity. That the modern function of this asymmetrical set of titles is indeed related to asymmetry in the basis for female and male social identity is further supported by the practice in 'polite society' of referring to women not only by their husband's family names, but by their given names as well (Stannard, 1977). Nilson (1977c) recounts the following bemusing experience:

> I looked through a standard desk-sized dictionary for ways we treat men and women differently, and was surprised to find what appears to be an attitude on the part of editors that

it is almost indecent to let a woman's name march unaccompanied across the pages of a dictionary. A woman's name must somehow be escorted by a male's name, regardless of whether he in his own right was as famous as the woman. For example, Charlotte Brontë was identified as Mrs Arthur B. Nicholls, Amelia Earhart was identified as Mrs George Palmer Putnam, Helen Hayes was identified as Mrs Charles McArthur, Zena Gale was identified as Mrs William Llywelyn Breese, and Jenny Lind was identified as Mme Otto Goldschmidt. [p. 138]

It is possible, of course, that social change will soon make these practices archaic. This issue is the topic of chapter 8.

Other forms of address

We have a variety of means at our disposal for addressing someone directly without using their personal names, of course. Terms like *ma'am, sir, dear, honey, love, duckie, sweetie, buddy, mack, fella* and *mate* are more or less familiar to people in different parts of the English-speaking world. The study of what these different forms signify and how they are used has been a fruitful source of information about the relationships between individuals and groups.

Brown (1965), for example, draws together historical and contemporary evidence to show how patterns of address may be used to signify complex interpersonal relations. He suggests that all interpersonal relations can be characterized in terms of at least two underlying dimensions, status and solidarity. The status dimension of a relationship is conditioned by the degree to which individuals differ in the possession of characteristics that are valued in society. The solidarity dimension relates to the degree of concern individuals feel for each other, which could range from none to a great deal.

Brown illustrates the influence of these two dimensions on speakers' choices of pronouns of address in European languages possessing formal and familiar pronouns for the second person singular. Speakers of French, for example, can select either the formal pronoun *vous* or the informal pronoun *tu* to address one another. In French and other languages with similar pronoun systems (called T/V systems), such as German and Spanish, the status dimension of a relationship was historically reflected by whether speakers addressed each other with the same pronoun or with different pronouns. Speakers of similar status would adopt the same pronoun, while speakers of clearly different status would adopt an asymmetrical pattern of address, with higher-status individuals using the T form and persons of lower status using the V form, to denote respect. This custom imposed some constraints on the expression of solidarity. Among speakers of similar status, there was no problem: the T form was used reciprocally to express solidarity, and the V form was used otherwise. However, for speakers of different status, the expression of solidarity via pronouns posed problems as long as the dimension of status took precedence in determining that an asymmetrical pattern of address must be used.

Essentially, the pronoun system was not complex enough to handle all possible combinations of status and solidarity simultaneously. This may not have been much of a practical problem during historical periods when the opportunity for solidary relationships depended mostly on people's status, as perhaps in feudal Europe. But as systems of rigid social stratification came under the challenge of the new political ideals of egalitarianism and social democracy, the solidarity function of the pronoun system seems gradually to have gained priority over the status function. In most of modern Europe, the use of the T or V form depends mainly on intimacy or familiarity and is largely blind to status distinctions, except in a few institutionalized and ritualized contexts.

What, you may ask, has all of this got to do with relations between the sexes among speakers of English, who do not have a T/V system at their disposal? Brown's analysis is important to us for several reasons that have nothing to do with his particular choice of the T/V system to illustrate his points. The same points could have been illustrated, although maybe not as conveniently, by reference to other forms of address.

First, the analysis sensitizes us to the potential significance of this aspect of lexical choice in conveying complex social messages. In the context of female–male relations, for example,

Kramer (1975) reports the results of a survey in which female and male students recorded over 500 instances of the way they were addressed by others in encounters with service personnel such as waiters and clerks. Women reported a wider range of address forms, varying from the respectful *ma'am,* to the informal *dear, honey* and *sweetie.* Males reported being addressed primarily as *sir,* sometimes as *dear* by female service personnel. Wolfson and Manes (1980) analysed address responses made to women in over 800 similar encounters, and discovered that the great majority fell into one of three major types: the traditional respect form, *ma'am*; the use of an informal term of endearment such as *honey* or *dear*; and what they call 'zero-form', or the use of no overt form of address at all. They describe several specific examples of regional individual and situational differences in the use of these forms, and make the interesting observation that the respectful and familiar forms are sometimes both used by the service person during the same episode.

It would be very interesting to have some hard evidence as to what people mean to signify when they use these terms, and how they are understood by the addressee. In the absence of such information, however, it seems likely that variations in these forms are intended more to indicate degrees of solidarity than degree of status. The possibility remains, however, that people can play upon the ambiguity of these forms in order to attain some control over the relationship. In this respect it is interesting that, on the basis of limited male data and casual observation, Wolfson and Manes (1980) suggest that the use of endearment forms with male clients is less frequent overall and the condition of their occurrence is quite different than for females.

Second, Brown's analysis also serves to warn us that the full significance of address forms may be revealed only when we know what forms they elicit in return. Thus, as suggestive as the studies described above may be, they provide us with insufficient evidence to be able to conclude simply that women and men are addressed differently. One would want to know more about the antecedent conditions of the forms that were observed (for example, do men and women open encounters with service personnel in the same way?) and about the way in which addressees respond to address forms of different types (for example, do women and men implicitly encourage and discourage different forms of address?).

A third important point that Brown makes in his analysis is that relationships between people are complex and multifaceted. In fact, recent research into the psychology of interpersonal relations lends support to Brown's characterization of such relations in terms of status and solidarity. Similar dimensions, more recently called 'control' and 'affiliation', emerge in the results of studies of personality structure (Kiesler, 1983; Wiggins, 1980, 1982), social interaction (c.g. Wish, D'Andrade and Goodnow, 1980) and communications (Miller, 1982). The ways in which these and other aspects of relations between the sexes as individuals and as groups are communicated is a matter to which I shall return in chapter 7.

Talking about Men and Women

Agent nouns

People often refer to themselves and others using nouns that describe an occupation or the performance of an activity, such as *author, actor, professor, plumber, jeweller, minister* and so on. It seems clear that the great majority of such terms more readily evoke the image of a man than of a women. Eakins and Eakins (1978) illustrate this point with the following riddle:

> A man and his young son were apprehended in a robbery. The father was shot during the struggle and the son, in handcuffs, was rushed to the police station. As the police pulled the struggling boy into the station, the mayor, who had been called to the scene, looked up and said, 'My God, it's my son!'. What relation was the mayor to the boy?

They report that most people offer wild and ridiculous guesses as to the solution, and that few people come up with the answer that the mayor was the boy's mother. This kind of riddle could be used as a simple test of degree to which a particular occupation or activity was more strongly associated with males or females. A similar kind of test can be made by pairing the word *male* and then the word *female* with each of a variety of occupations or activity nouns, and judging each of the resulting combinations for redundancy or repetitiveness (e.g. *male plumber–female plumber; male nurse–female nurse; male sailor–female sailor*). I would predict that many more of the word pairs that include the word *male* will be judged repetitious than will pairs that include the word *female*.

The reasons for this asymmetry in the semantic connotations of agent nouns are undoubtedly social, and have little to do directly with the ultimate etymological origins of the words themselves (Miller and Swift, 1976). Yet this has not prevented eminent lexicographers from encouraging us to invent and adopt alternate forms of these nouns when referring to women: terms like *authoress, actress, aviatrix* and so on. Feminists have argued that the addition of diminutive suffixes to agent nouns results in terms that have less semantic potency than their unaltered counterparts, and that this both causes and reflects a devaluation of those who occupy these agentive roles. This is certainly an issue that requires some empirical attention, but in the meantime we may simply note that the creation of special terms for women who perform the functions described by agent nouns is unparsimonious and confusing, and is not paralleled for males who occupy traditionally female roles.

The owner and the owned

Lakoff (1975) argues that men are defined in terms of what they do in the world, while women are defined in terms of the men with whom they are associated, a principle to which we have alluded above. Eakins and Eakins (1976) paraphrase this principle in terms of the owner and the owned, and suggest that women more often than men are referred to in terms of their partners: 'John's wife', 'Harry's daughter', 'Bill's girlfriend' and so on. They argue that, while this discrepancy can be observed at all stages in the life-cycle, both before and after marriage, it becomes most acute in the event of a spouse's death: 'A woman whose husband dies is "Ed's widow". But the man whose wife is deceased is not commonly referred to as "Vera's widower" ' (p. 117).

Word order

Another asymmetry in the representation of women and men in language is reflected in the order of precedence given to males and females when they are referred to together. It seems that the old maxim 'Ladies before gentlemen', is more often honoured in the breach than in the observance. Readers may have noticed that I have alternated the order of female and male, man and woman, when they have appeared together in the same sentence, and you will have to ask yourself the degree to which this jars your sensibilities, and why. A list of other common female-male pairings is given below in their usual word order. You might like to devise a test to verify that this really *is* the more expected order:

> husband and wife
> son and daughter
> brother and sister
> host and hostess
> king and queen
> Adam and Eve

In fact, little is known about the social or psychological significance of the order of word pairs like this, and the fact that women often come second may or may not signify to the listener that they have less status or importance than the male. If the connotations of other ordered word pairs are anything to go by though (e.g. *good–bad; rich–poor; day–night; light–dark; big– little; life–death*), the hypothesis may be valid. The phenomenon of word order does not stand alone; and, in conjunction with the other asymmetries that have been described above and will be described below, it contributes to an overall picture of the ways in which the sexes are represented as being not just descriptively different but also evaluatively different.

Semantic degeneration

From an historical point of view the words in each of the

following pairs are synonymous with respect to the role or function that they describe:

king	queen
governor	governess
lord	lady
mister	mistress
patron	matron
sir	madam
bachelor	spinster

It is clear however that these words are not synonymous when it comes to other dimensions of meaning in contemporary usage. None of the feminine terms in the list connotes the same degree of strength or power as its masculine counterpart, and almost all of them have acquired secondary sexual connotations. Lexicographers have noted that, once a word or term becomes associated with women, it often acquires semantic characteristics that are congruent with social stereotypes and evaluations of women as a group, a process that has variously been termed 'semantic derogation' (Shulz, 1975), 'semantic degeneration' (Miller and Swift, 1976) and 'semantic polarization' (Eakins and Eakins, 1978).

He/Man Language

Of all the referential asymmetries that pertain to the female-male domain, none has attracted more attention and controversy than the practice of using nouns and pronouns that are marked for masculinity (*man, mankind, he, him, his*) when referring to people in a general sense, and to individuals of unknown or idefinite sex. These practices, about which many excellent papers have recently been written (Bodine, 1975; Martyna, 1980; McConnell-Ginet, 1979; Miller and Swift, 1976; Stanley, 1976), have their linguistic and social history buried deep in the past. However, some fragments of this history may help us to understand more about these practices today.

Generic nouns

Generic nouns perform the very useful function of allowing us to refer to an entire class of entities with a single word, and most if not all languages have one or more forms that can be used to designate members of the human species in general. Among speakers of Old English, prior to AD 1000, the term *man* was apparently used exclusively in the generic sense. The terms *wif* and *wer* denoted females and males respectively. Gradually, by means of processes about which we can only speculate, the form *man* took over the semantic duty that had been performed by *wer* while still retaining its alternate generic function, resulting in its modern meaning.

One reason for the recent attention surrounding this term is the growth of awareness about the portrait of the social order implied in its etymological history – in which the male half of the species, whose members dominate and even define the public domain, contrive to co-opt for their own special purpose the generic term. 'One cannot help but wonder', as do Miller and Swift (1976), 'what would have happened to the word that originally meant a human being if females rather than males had dominated the society in which English evolved through its first thousand years' (p. 28).

An equally important source of concern, however, is the ambiguity of a term that stands for both an entire class and a specific subset of the class, and the opportunity for misuse and misunderstanding that this presents. Graham (1975) observes:

> If a woman is swept off a ship into the water, the cry is 'Man overboard!' If she is killed by a hit-and-run driver, the charge is 'manslaughter'! If she is injured on the job, the coverage is 'workman's compensation'! But if she arrives at a threshold marked 'Men Only', she knows the admonition is not intended to bar animals or plants or inanimate objects. It is meant for her. [p. 62]

And Miller and Swift (1976), always the observant critics, comment:

Writing in a national magazine, the psychoanalyst Erich Fromm described man's 'vital interests' as 'life, food, access to females, etc.' One may be saddened but not surprised at the statement 'man is the only primate that commits rape'. Although, as commonly understood, it can apply to only half the human population, it is nevertheless semantically acceptable. But, 'man, being a mammal, breast-feeds his young' is taken as a joke. [pp. 25. 26]

To test the hypotheses that *man* is understood in the generic sense, Schneider and Hacker (1973) asked college students to select magazine and newspaper pictures to illustrate the chapter topics in a sociology textbook. Among students who were given titles using the generic *man* (such as *social man, urban man* and *economic man*), 64 per cent of the pictures submitted showed only men. Titles without the generic (*social behaviour, urban behaviour,* etc.) elicited only 50 per cent of male-only submissions (see also Harrison, 1975). The last word on this particular issue goes to Miller and Swift (1976):

> Those who have grown up with a language that tells them they are at the same time men and not men are faced with ambivalence – not about their sex, but about their status as human beings. For the question 'Who is man?' it seems is a political one, and the very ambiguity of the word is what makes it a useful tool for those who have a stake in maintaining the status quo. [pp. 37, 38]

Generic pronouns

The emergence of the generic *he* probably correlates with the extension of the meaning of *man* in English. However, prior to the insistence of prescriptive grammarians from the nineteenth century that *he* is the only 'correct' form of grammatical reference to a singular sex-indefinite antecedent, the alternative forms *he or she* and singular *they* were common and accepted (Bodine, 1975). The situation then paralleled the current situation concerning generic *man*: alternatives were available and were used, and one might have enquired as to the reasons for the absence of a generic *she*. From the middle of the nineteenth century until very recently, however, the situation became progressively more polarized as the prescriptive grammarians attempted to legislate *he or she* and singular *they* out of existence. Bodine (1975) confirmed the impact of the prescriptive movement on contemporary educational practice in a survey of 33 school grammar books, 28 of which explicitly condemned the alternatives: *he or she* because it is clumsy, and singular *they* because it is incorrect.

From a strictly grammatical point of view, the argument that *he or she* is clumsy or awkward is irrelevant, although most people would probably agree with the objection from a stylistic point of view. But what of the charge that singular *they* is incorrect? The answer depends upon what one takes as the criterion of grammaticality. On the basis of a formal analysis of the pronoun system in which *they* is only plural in meaning, the accused is guilty as charged. But if one's gramaticality criterion is variable, and based upon observations of use and judgement, then the issue becomes an empirical one: do people use the singular *they* and judge it to be acceptable?

We will return to this issue below. More to the point of the present discussion are the questions surrounding the use of the generic *he*. From a formalistic point of view, generic *he* is open to the objection that it fails to agree with the grammatical gender of a singular sex-indefinite antecedent, and is thus grammatically inadequate by one feature – the same number as the singular *they*, which fails to agree with its antecedent in terms of number. These and other observations (Bodine, 1975) provide a convincing argument that the exhortations of prescriptive grammarians concerning the use of generic *he* can be seen as little more than sophisticated rationalizations for a socially motivated language change, a change once again reflecting, in form, aspects of the arrangement between the sexes.

As with *man* and its compounds, however, socio-historical issues are only part of the reason for contemporary interest in generics. Of equal if not greater importance is the need to know how *he* is presently used and understood.

Writers often undermine the probability that generics will serve a generic function by making sex-specific references in the same passage (Stanley, 1976). Moreover, evidence from several experiments indicates that the generic *he* is not always understood to include both sexes, even in contexts that are explicitly designed to facilitate this interpretation, much less in more ambiguous contexts. Martyna (1980) reports the results of two experiments in which students were asked to judge, in a series of consecutive trials, whether pictures of either a male or a female could apply to sentences containing generic *he, they* or *he-or-she.* While male pictures were judged unequivocally to be applicable to sentences containing all generic forms, and female pictures to be applicable to sentences containing *they* or *he-or-she,* 20 per cent of the students in one experiment and 40 per cent in a second one judged female pictures not to apply to sentences containing the generic *he*!

MacKay and Fulkerson (1979) describe some similar experiments. In the first, students were asked to indicate whether sentences containing sex-specific nouns (e.g. 'The front door was quickly answered by his *aunt*') or pronouns (e.g. 'An old housekeeper cleaned *her* carpet before sunrise') or the generic *he* (e.g. 'A bicyclist can bet that *he* is not safe from dogs') could refer to one or more *females.* Errors in comprehension of the sex-specific sentences occurred at the rate of only 2 per cent. 'Errors' in comprehension of the sentences containing generic *he* occurred 87 per cent of the time! These results are all the more significant when we consider that among the generic stimuli were included sentences with predominantly feminine antecedents (e.g. *secretary, typist, receptionist, model*) as well as those with neutral and masculine antecedents. The sex-related connotations of the antecedent did not significantly influence the interpretation of the generic *he.* Subsequent experiments (see also MacKay, 1980) support the conclusion that *he* overwhelmingly tends to be comprehended as sex-specific, even in supposedly generic contexts, and in contexts doctored to encourage the perception of females.

Examining the production of pronouns, Martyna (1980) recruited 400 students ranging from kindergarten to college-aged to complete sentence fragments that contained references to singular sex-indefinite antecedents in male-related, female-related and neutral roles. Martyna reasoned that, if *he* is an adequate generic term, then it will be used whenever a pronoun must be chosen without knowing the sex of the referent. As you will have anticipated, the results did not support this view of the generic *he*. Ninety-six per cent of the male-related sentences were completed with *he*, 87 per cent of the female-related sentences were completed with *she*, and 65 per cent of the neutral sentences were completed with *he*. Alternatives, which included *they* and *he-or-she*, were used in 30 per cent of the neutral sentences and about 5 per cent of the others. It is clear that, in spite of the best efforts of prescriptive grammarians, *he* has not come to be either used or understood in the generic sense under most circumstances.

Metaphorical Themes in the Sexual Subculture

As was mentioned at the outset of this chapter, there have been many attempts to distil the essence of asymmetries in the representation of the arrangement between the sexes into contrasts that purport to describe the major dimensions of the sexual subculture. The final section of this chapter introduces several of the more salient of these themes.

The discussion is meant to be not definitive, but only illustrative. Important themes have undoubtedly been overlooked – indeed, the richness of the gender formulae ensures that no list of contrasts will ever be complete. However, this should not discourage us from attempting to ascertain the dominant organizational principles that structure our beliefs and behaviours as participants in the sexual subculture.

It is evident that many of the themes discussed below are under severe stress in today's society, and may no longer represent the beliefs of major segments of the population. But there is little doubt that until recently these themes were all endowed with an air of legitimacy, and they continue to be the point of departure for discussion and critique today. It is also important to bear in mind that we are not here concerned to describe what men and women are actually like, but rather to determine what the norms of masculinity and femininity expect and encourage us to be like.

I have organized these themes into three categories: (1) those that pertain to personal qualities held to be part of the individual psychological makeup of every woman or man; (2) those that relate to expected differences in the conduct of men and women in interpersonal relations; and (3) those that are applied to women and men as groups in society.

At the individual level, perhaps the most pervasive organizational theme is the equation of masculinity with rationality and objectivity, and of femininity with emotionality and subjectivity. Where men are seen to be slaves to the dictates of logic and reason, women are captives to affection and passion. Women are also supposed to be weak and timid; men, strong and brave. A great variety of other stereotypically masculine and feminine personal qualities emerge in studies of sex stereotypes, many of which will be revealed in chapters 4–7. One of the more interesting features of these schemes is that they are not always internally consistent. For example, in a study of stereotypes described in chapter 5, men were rated as both more rational and more reckless, and women as more soft-spoken and more nagging (see p. 108).

At the interpersonal level, the most salient theme is captured in Bakan's (1966) quasi-philosophical discussion of the quality of human nature in terms of the masculine principle of 'agency', which implies a sense of self and a tendency towards self-assertion, and the feminine principle of selfless concern for others, which he calls 'communion'. This expansive distinction largely subsumes an earlier equation of masculinity with 'instrumentality' and femininity with 'expressiveness' (Parsons and Bales, 1955). Empirical support for these intuitive formulations comes from many studies of sex stereotypes which find that men are believed to be more egocentric, dominant, competitive and aggressive, while women are held to be more sensitive, warm, appreciative and helpful (see chapter 7). Recent research on the dimensions of interpersonal orientation and conduct has led to the use of the terms 'dominance' and 'control' to refer to the agency dimension and 'nurturance' and 'affiliation' to refer to the dimension of communion (e.g. Kiesler, 1983; Wiggins, 1982). The links between the personal themes of rationality and emotionality on one hand, and the interpersonal themes of control and affiliation on the other, are easily seen. In chapter 7 the impact of these themes on interpersonal communication will be explicitly examined.

At the group level, the theme that emerges most clearly from the material reviewed in this chapter is the equation of men and masculinity with normalcy (in both a descriptive and prescriptive sense), and the equation of women and femininity with deviance. Thus, men and men's attributes and activities serve as the standard against which the virtues of all human attributes and activities are measured. This is easily exposed in the less-than-subtle instance of the evolution and use of the generic masculine, the encoding of agent nouns, and perhaps too in the under-representation of women in the media and reference material. The assumption operates in the tendency among social scientists to devote attention to the description of 'women's speech' or 'women's behaviour' as a special topic (e.g. Jespersen, 1922; Lakoff, 1975; for commentary see Kramarae, 1981; Spender, 1980). As we shall see in chapter 4, much has been made of the fact that women show more pronunciation changes from informal to formal interview contexts than do men, a pattern that has been labelled 'hypercorrection' (Labov, 1966). This label clearly characterizes sex differences in contextual sensitivity in terms of deviation from a male standard. Other examples are rife in social scientific writing, and sensitize us to the fact that even the most innocuous, 'descriptive' practices may unintentionally reinforce the status quo.

The normal–deviant theme correlates with but is not identical to several other important contrasts, all of which contribute uniquely to the representation of women and men as social categories. Several of these converge to lend a vertical structure to the arrangement between the sexes. Women are not accorded the same social status as men, in spite of laws designed to prevent sex-based discrimination. Men are seen to have more social power than women, power that is believed to derive from physical, personal and interpersonal sources. In fact, the application of a majority–minority metaphor to the domain of male–female relations has been made quite successfully (for discussion see Kramarae, 1981; Williams and Giles, 1978).

These asymmetries are sometimes seen to have antecedents in the horizontal structure of the arrangement between the sexes, to which attention is drawn by the contrasts political–domestic and public–private. Women are encouraged to be responsible for the integrity of the domestic sphere of life, including working at home and caring for children. Since most of this activity is devoted to maintaining the nuclear family, women are not as easily thought of as active participants in the sphere of public debate and political decision-making. Men, on the other hand, work away from home, where they can easily associate with other men for the purpose of debating and defining everything from the policy for the 'common good' to the 'meaning of life'.

It is the consequences of this asymmetry in role-related expectations and activity, especially for women, that have led to the most poignant and controversial metaphors. Perhaps the most familiar of these is the theme oppressor-oppressed, which goes beyond the high status–low status and majority–minority metaphors in attributing intent and responsibility to men for the plight of women. Arguments about the form and precise consequences of women's oppression vary greatly, as anyone who is familiar with the women's movement and feminist thought will be aware. Here I will simply draw attention to the communication-related theme that has evolved from this superordinate formulation. Men, in their dominant public roles, are seen not only to control access to public forums and communications resources, but even to control the conventions according to which experience is defined and articulated. Men are seen to be dominant: women are perceived to be muted, and one consequence may be that they find it difficult to gain access to the conceptual tools that would enable them to articulate their experience and change their position. Men are the namers, women, the named (see Spender, 1980).

Irrespective of the absolute validity of any or all of these themes when measured against the objective social arrangement between the sexes, there can be little doubt that they feature prominently in representations of them. Of course, not one of these contrasts pertains exclusively to the representation of female-male relations. The meaning of each one, the aspects of social life that it reminds us of or sensitizes us to, probably stems from many different sources (Strathern, 1976; MacCormack and Strathern, 1980).

We can also take a leaf from the book of those who argue that sex differences in speech are due more to differences between women and men in the social niches that they typically occupy than to intrinsic sex differences (see chapter 7). The division of labour between the sexes has undoubtedly led to an unequal distribution of men and women in most occupational and other social domains. Furthermore, the activities of women and men in these domains are usually different. Different activity types and the situations in which they usually occur are undoubtedly imbued with colourful connotations, supposed to capture their essential qualities. It would not be surprising if the categories of people stereotypically associated with different kinds of social activity acquire the labels that are used to describe their situations. At the most general level, then, it may be that some of the themes mentioned above originate with descriptions of situations and activities, and become sex-associated as a consequence of beliefs about (and the realities of) a sexual division of labour. We will return to examine this further in chapter 7.

4

Feminine and Masculine Speech

The Recognition of Speaker Sex

Some combination of physical and fashion-related cues appear to qualify as the criteria for distinguishing between men and women under normal circumstances. Furthermore, there seems to be almost unanimous agreement about these criteria. Indeed, it is only because of this consensus that we can use Goffman's notion of the sexual subculture as a shorthand for a culture-wide system of social organization.

Ordinarily, speech and language variables do not figure prominently as cues to sexual classification. Occasionally, though, when speaking on the telephone or listening to the radio, speech may be the only available clue to someone's sex. As will be described below, even masked and filtered speech elicits reliable, highly consensual and generally accurate judgements of speaker sex.

Prepubertal speaker sex recognition

Human vocalizations produce electromagnetic energy in the form of sound, which is distributed unevenly in bands along the audible spectrum. The perceived pitch of the human voice is tied closely, but not exactly, to the average frequency with which the vocal chords vibrate, that is the *laryngeal fundamental frequency* (abbreviated f_0), which is measured in cycles per second, or hertz (Hz). Roughly speaking, an increase of 100 per cent in f_0 results in a perceived increase in vocal pitch of one octave on the musical scale (Luchsinger and Arnold, 1965).

The international standard tone for tuning musical instruments is 400 Hz, or middle A. Coincidentally, this is also the average f_0 of newborn infants' usual response to their arrival, termed the 'reflex phonation' (Luchsinger and Arnold, 1965) and more popularly known as the 'birth cry'. Gutzman and Flatau (1906) arrived at this figure after recording and analysing the first cries, the result of a reflexive inspiration and exhalation of air, of 30 neonates. More recent studies reveal a tendency for boys between three and six days of age to have a higher average crying f_0 than girls of the same age (449.5 Hz average for boys, compared with 416.9 Hz average for girls: Murray, Amundson and Hollien, 1977). Nevertheless, the trend is statistically insignificant, and at any rate mothers cannot reliably distinguish between male and female infants on the basis of cries alone (Murray, Hollien and Muller, 1975).

As children grow older, their voices develop and their vocal ranges increase. These changes are determined by the growth of their vocal chords, which lengthen and thicken at much the same rate as body height and weight increase. Very little is known about pitch markers of sex between infancy and puberty, although it is generally accepted that, for children of the same weight and height, f_0 should not differ significantly (Sachs, 1975). Since boys enjoy a slight average size advantage over girls from birth (Tanner, 1978), corresponding average differences in f_0 might be expected.

Yet f_0 is not the only important pitch-related characteristic of the human voice. The sound produced by the larynx resonates at characteristic frequencies in the various cavities (throat, nose and mouth) of the vocal tract, producing bands of acoustic energy known as 'formants' (cf. Peterson and Barney, 1952). The interaction of f_0 and the pressure at which air is driven through the larynx, together with the anatomical shape and posture of the vocal cavities, determines the sound of the formants. These sounds are perceptually associated with aspects of 'voice quality', including vowel sounds and, importantly in this context, the timbre of the voice. Characteristic individual formant frequencies are commonly derived by having a person produce sustained vowel sounds, and finding the average frequency of each formant band.

Vocal tract resonance information is more likely to lead to correct identifications of the sex of pre-pubertal children than f_0. Weinberg and Bennett (1971) recorded samples of spontaneous speech from 66 five- and six-year-old girls and boys and found that judges were able to identify correctly the sex of the speaker 74 per cent of the time, even though the mean f_0 of the sexes did not differ significantly. Similarly, Sachs, Lieberman and Erickson (1973) recorded the same sentence of speech from each of 26 boys and girls aged between four and twelve years. Listeners' accuracy in the identification of the speaker sex was 81 per cent, even though the average f_0 of the boys in the sample was somewhat higher than that of the girls.

Weinberg and Bennett (1971) hypothesized that boys in their sample of speakers might have had slightly larger vocal tracts than the girls, noting that the boys were on average somewhat bigger. The anatomical size of the vocal tract cavities is highly correlated with the overall size of the child, and appears to be the main determinant of formant frequencies. Yet Sachs, Lieberman and Erickson (1973), whose speakers consisted of children of a variety of weights and heights, reasoned that the accuracy of sex identification in their study was based on more than either f_0 or formant frequencies alone, since otherwise all small children should have been identified as girls, and larger children as boys (which did not happen). Apparently, listeners were able to infer the general size of the children before making decisions about their sex. They drew on a suggestion offered by Mattingly (1966) to account for his discovery that the separation between adult men and women in the distribution of formants was greater than that expected on the basis of variability in vocal tract size alone. The cavities of the vocal tract can be modified in size and shape by movements of the head, throat, jaws, lips and tongue, and Mattingly suggested that women and men alter vocal characteristics by means of such modifications to conform to feminine and masculine vocal 'archetypes', or stereotypes, in the terminology of this review.

Sachs, Lieberman and Erikson (1973) decided to investigate the possibility that the average formant frequency differences between the sexes are accentuated by sex-associated modifications to the vocal tract; and they measured the first and second formants, usually the most acoustically informative, of three vowels for nine boy–girl pairs of children matched for height and weight. The formants were significantly lower in the case of boys for two of the vowels. Furthermore, the voices that had most consistently been judged masculine had lower formants than those rated as more girl-like.

In a further attempt to locate the critical cues to speaker sex identification among the children in her sample, Sachs (1975) played tapes of (1) the isolated vowels, and (2) the spoken sentences played backwards, to a new group of listeners. In condition (1) the overall accuracy was 60 per cent, significantly reduced from the 81 per cent correct with normal sentences. This indicated the importance of either the additional phonetic information contained in the sentences, or the temporal information associated with intonation, speech rate, fluency, etc. For condition (2), when the sentences were played backwards confusing the normal temporal cues, accuracy dropped to 59 per cent, a figure that is not significantly above chance performance.

These studies demonstrate that speech provides fairly reliable and accurate criteria for sexual classification, even when those being judged are children. In other words, the link between vocal sex stereotypes and vocal sex differences is strong. Yet, however direct such a link might be, and whatever the combination of speech variables that evokes attributions of sex to pre-pubertal children, it is evident that listeners are not reacting to sex differences *per se*. If they were, the identification of speaker sex would be perfect, which it is not: in these studies typically between one-fifth and one-quarter of the children are mis-categorized on the basis of speech.

It remains possible that listeners are responding to anatomical and maturational factors that are only secondarily, but still closely, associated with sex, although Sachs's (1975) tentative confirmation of Mattingly's (1966) hypothesis about the accentuation of formant differences between the sexes casts doubt on this being the only source of variation. It also seems improbable that the sentential cues that Sachs showed were so important could be the result of intra-individual biological sex differences. On the basis of what is currently known, it is at least as plausible to hypothesize that pre-pubertal children are encouraged to conform to sex-associated behavioural norms, which encompass speech behaviour among many other things.

There is ample evidence that adults have different attitudes towards and expectations of boys and girls from the day that the children are born. Rubin, Provenzano and Luria (1974) presented a rating scale questionnnaire to the parents of 30 neonates, 15 boys and 15 girls. Although the mean size, weight and developmental level of the children of each sex did not differ, parents – especially fathers – rated daughters as being cuter, prettier and smaller and sons as stronger, hardier, better co-ordinated. In a somewhat similar study (Seavy, Katz and Zalk, 1975), non-parent subjects were observed interacting with a three-month old infant. One-third of the adult volunteers were told that 'Baby X' was a boy, one-third were told that the baby was a girl, and one-third were given no information as to the infant's sex. During a three-minute period of unobtrusive observation, the reactions of each subject to the infant were recorded and rated under several categories of response. The complex results of the study indicated, among other things, that adults interacted differently with the same infant (who was in reality a girl), depending on whether they thought it was a girl or a boy. For example, a plastic doll was chosen as an appropriate toy with which to amuse the 'girl' infant more often than either a toy football or a teething ring, which were chosen more often for the 'boy' infant.

In another study of the effect of sex-related preconceptions on the general interpretation of infant behaviour, Condry and Condry (1976) asked university students to watch a videotape of a nine-month old infant responding to repeated presentations of each of four stimuli (a teddy bear, a jack-in-the-box, a doll and a buzzer). Subjects were asked to rate the intensity of the child's emotional response to each stimulus on three scales: for pleasure, anger and fear. Some subjects were told that the infant was a boy, and the rest were told that it was a girl (the real sex of the child is not disclosed in the article). Although all subjects saw the same videotape, subjects in the 'boy' condition rated the child as showing more pleasure across all situations. More significantly, the child's startled responses to the jack-in-the-box were interpreted as 'anger' when the infant was labelled as a boy and 'fear' when it was labelled as a girl. After they had seen the videotape, subjects completed nine semantic differential rating scales on the infant, measuring activity, potency and evaluative dimensions (Osgood, Suci and Tannenbaum, 1957). Subjects in the two experimental conditions rated the infant as equally good, but subjects who saw the 'boy' rated him as slightly but significantly more active and potent than subjects who saw the 'girl'.

More directly pertinent to the domain of speech, Lieberman (1967) has noted that mothers and fathers speak differently to children, and that children may react to this by shifting their pitch in an attempt to match that of the parent. Furthermore, parents speak differently to male and female children in terms of both the purpose of the interaction (Cherry and Lewis, 1975) and the situations when interaction will be initiated (Wells, 1979).

Berko-Gleason (1978) speculates that these differences in expectation and treatment do influence the child's acquisition of communicative routines, but she points out that the direction of causal influences is probably not one-way. Adults' expectations of child sex difference in language may be based in part on fact, since even neonate girls and boys differ on some measures of activity and reactivity (Baumel and Lewis, 1971; Bell and Darling, 1965; Weller and Bell, 1965). In sum, one must agree with Berko-Gleason (1978) that sex differences in language pertaining to behaviour reviewed in this and subsequent chapters 'arises out of a complex interaction between children with particular endowments and parents, with all of the expectations, special ways of speaking, and patterns of sensitivity' (p. 156). However, the perspicacity of this conclusion is matched at present only by our ignorance of the nature of the interaction.

Post-pubertal speaker sex recognition

At the age of about 12 years in girls and a couple of years later in boys, the adolescent growth spurt produces numerous physical changes, including rapid maturation of the vocal chords. Although this process begins earlier in females than in males, the changes in men's speaking apparatus are more marked, resulting in an average length increase of 10 cm (bringing an average total length of 23 cm) as compared with only 3–4 cm in females (average total length = 17 cm). Fundamental frequency appears to be closely linked to the length of the vocal chords, and the pubertal growth spurt probably accounts for much of the difference between adult men's and women's f_0, which can be estimated to be 90–100 Hz for normal speakers in the United States. Hollien and Shipp (1972), reporting data from 175 males between the ages of 20 and 89, found an average f_0 of around 115 Hz up to the age of 70, where a significant increase in pitch occurred, and was accentuated in the 80–90-year-old group (mean f_0 = 146 Hz). Normative studies of female speakers (McGlone, Hollien and Moore, 1965) result in an average of about 210 Hz, or one octave higher than men. Unlike men, women do not show increased pitch in old age (McGlone and Hollien, 1963).

Several investigators have tried to ascertain the acoustical cues necessary and sufficient for the accurate identification of adult speaker sex. The association between sex and perceived pitch is well-established, and f_0 is probably the single most important cue. Nevertheless, the association accounts for only part of the average variation between women's and men's voices, and cannot of itself explain our almost perfect capacity to discriminate between adult women and adult men on the basis of speech alone. Schwartz (1968) and Ingeman (1968) recorded men and women producing isolated voiceless fricatives (speech sounds such as /h/, /s/ and /f/, which do not have a laryngeal component) and obtained close to 100 per cent accuracy of identification. Schwartz and Rine (1968) had men and women record two whispered vowels and again obtained almost perfect accuracy of identification. Listeners in these studies could only have been responding on the basis of perceptions associated with vocal tract resonance, since laryngeal vibration is not necessary to produce these speech sounds.

Coleman (1971) found that sex identification from laryngeal speech, which is voiceless speech driving an electronic larynx, was more than 80 per cent accurate, even though f_0 was set at a constant 85 Hz. Furthermore, the judgements of speaker sex correlated highly with the speaker's average formant frequency ($r = 0.70$). It appears that the characteristics of vocal tract resonance are potent determinants of accurate speaker sex identification, in addition to f_0, and Mattingly's (1966) findings of between-sex accentuation of formant differences is important in the adult context.

Two investigators have attempted to tease apart the relative importance of laryngeal fundamental frequency and vocal tract resonance information. Coleman (1976) created a series of 'ambiguous' voices by having 10 speakers, with vocal tract resonances at the extremes of those measured in 40 adults, record a passage while articulating by means of a variable frequency laryngeal vibrator. For one series of recordings, f_0 was set at the typically masculine frequency of 120 Hz, and for the other series f_0 was set at 240 Hz, which is typically feminine. Masculine f_0 was perceptually dominant as a determinant of speaker sex judgements, even when combined with female vocal tract cues. But the combination of female f_0 and masculine formant frequencies resulted in unreliable attributions of speaker sex. Of the two variable factors in this study, variation in f_0 produced more reliable variations in listeners' judgements than changes in formant information. However, the dichotomous synthetic manipulation of f_0 may have contributed artificially to its salience.

In a later study, Lass et al. (1976) recorded 10 women and 10 men producing six isolated vowel sounds in a normal speaking voice and in a whisper (thus providing only formant information). They made a third tape by filtering out the formant bandwidths from the normally voiced tape, leaving only f_0 information. The percentage of accurate judgements of speaker sex made by 15 female listeners were: 96 per cent for the normal voiced tape, 91 per cent for the filtered tape and 75 per cent for the whispered tape. Furthermore, listeners expressed, via rating scales, most confidence in their ratings of the normal tape and least confidence for the whispered tape. These findings confirm the relatively greater contribution of f_0 to accurate attributions of adult speaker sex, compared with resonance information, a pattern the reverse of that found for judgements of children's sex.

Moreover, temporal alteration of adult speech does not seem to affect the accuracy of identification adversely, as Sachs (1975) found that it did with children as speakers. Lass, Mertz and Kimmel (1978) recorded 10 men and 10 women each speaking four short sentences; and 30 female listeners judged the sex of the speakers from the original tape or from one of two experimental tapes, one of which was time-compressed to 40 per cent of the original recording time, while the other was the original tape played backwards. Speaker sex identification was nearly perfect for all three tapes.

The link between beliefs about vocal sex differences and actual sex differences is even stronger for adult speakers than for children. The anatomical substrate of these adult sex differences is much more clear-cut than it is for pre-pubertal speakers, although Mattingly's (1966) data suggest that anatomy is not the only reason for female–male vocal differences. Whether anatomy-related vocal differences or conformity to vocal sex stereotypes contributes more to listeners' ability to distinguish adult females from adult males on the basis of speech is a question that can be answered only after more research, possibly in several different cultural contexts.

Future directions

It is clear from the studies of Sachs (1975), Schwartz (1968), Schwartz and Rine (1968), Ingeman (1968), Coleman (1971, 1976) and Lass *et al.* (1976) that, when voice is the only source of information about a person's sex, categorization correlates highly with vocal tract resonance. However, almost all of the studies described above involve an experimental paradigm wherein linguistically naive listeners are required to judge the sex of the speakers from tape-recorded speech samples that have been altered in one of a number of ways so as to eliminate all but a specific set of vocal cues. This is potentially the ultimate test of whether or not some speech feature is stereotypically sex-associated, since listeners' judgements are based entirely upon their preconceptions about women's and men's typical speech. However, since researchers in this area have been concerned with speaker sex recognition, they have usually reported their results not in terms of features that elicit reliable and consensual listener judgements, but in terms of the proportion of judgements that are correct.

These accuracy scores are very useful from the point of view of being able to articulate the degree of overlap between sex stereotypes about vocal variables and actual sex differences. However, accuracy scores do not necessarily reflect the reliability of listeners' judgements. For example, listeners may be only 50 per cent accurate in their judgements of sex, yet they may be responding much more reliably or consensually than this figure would suggest, since consensual but inaccurate responses are not represented in accuracy scores. Thus, the speech cues that lead to reliable, even if inaccurate, judgements of sex will go undiscovered, and the precise nature of vocal sex stereotypes will remain obscure.

Only when accuracy is very high do accuracy scores by themselves give some indication of consensus on behalf of listeners about the masculine and feminine connotations of the speech variables under investigation. For example, accuracy at the rate of 75 per cent indicates at least this much listener consensus, although listeners could be responding with 100 per cent agreement and still be only 75 per cent accurate.

Accuracy scores in most of the experiments described in this chapter were over 75 per cent, indicating at least this much consensus. However, the diminished accuracy that accompanied temporal alterations in Sachs (1975) and whispering in Lass *et al.* (1976) cannot automatically be interpreted as being due to the absence of sex stereotypes for these variables. Reliable patterns of sex classification that were inaccurate would have gone undetected. Thus, while one can conclude that variations in either f_0 or vocal tract resonance are sufficient to evoke reliable masculinity and femininity attributions, one cannot conclude that they are necessary even in a 'vocal cues only' context. Minimal feminine and masculine vocal cues have yet to be discovered.

Finally, it is probable that the masculine and feminine overtones of speech variables, and for that matter any other sex stereotypical cues, derive from many sources outside the immediate context of female–male relations. For example, some authors have commented on the tough, masculine connotations of so-called working-class speech (e.g. Trudgill, 1975). An interesting study in this connection is one by Edwards (1979), who recorded 20 working-class and 20 middle-class ten-year-olds, balanced for sex, reading the same short passage. Fourteen student teachers judged the sex of each speaker, achieving an overall accuracy of 83.6 per cent. However, significantly more errors were made in the identification of working-class girls and middle-class boys than for the other speaker groups. Something about working-class speech skewed the judgements towards *male*, while the opposite effect operated for middle-class speakers. The voices were further rated by five listeners on some impressionistically speech-related scales, where working-class speakers were rated as having lower, rougher and more masculine voices overall.

It is very unlikely that vocal variables were the only speech cues influencing listeners' judgements in Edward's study, for a wide variety of very informative phenomena other than vocal variables are free to vary in content-controlled settings. Some of these possible sources of influence will be discussed in the next section.

Intonational and Paralinguistic Correlates of Perceived Femininity and Masculinity

Variations in the permanent and quasi-permanent characteristics of a person's voice appear to constitute a functionally valid basis for distinguishing women from men on average. However, given that there are normally more salient criteria available for the classification of sex, even the most sex-stereotypical speech cues probably figure less prominently in the process of social categorization than in the post-categorical process of inferring masculinity and femininity.

In this section two classes of speech phenomena that are closely related to vocal variables, but over which speakers have more obvious voluntary control, are discussed. These features, which along with vocal features are in principle quite independent of pronunciation and grammar, are modified during the course of an utterance to add affective and emphatic coloration to speech.

The first group to be discussed concerns the distribution of changes in pitch during an utterance. In English and other languages in which intonation is not an integral part of word meaning (in contrast to languages such as Chinese and Thai, where phonetically similar syllables pronounced with different inflections denote different concepts), changes in pitch are distributed in characteristic patterns over the course of the utterance. Studies from the United States and England suggest that women use a greater variety of intonational patterns than do men, and that intonational dynamism is stereotypically associated with femininity. Certain emotionally significant combinations of basic 'tones' have also been shown to elicit reliable judgements of masculinity and femininity. Once again, however, the purpose of these studies is primarily descriptive, and insight into the process underlying these judgements and their dynamics is notably absent.

The same must be said for the few studies of variables with a functional status and temporal order of magnitude similar to intonational features, also discussed here under the heading, 'paralinguistic variables'. The studies discussed in this section, while suggestive of a possible approach to the study of sex stereotypes associated with speech features, suffer from methodological shortcomings and generate data bases that are suggestive but too meagre to permit firm conclusions.

Masculine and feminine intonations

Intonational characteristics are a prominent feature of intuitive descriptons of typically masculine and feminine speech. Crystal (1971), for example, provides an impressionistic analysis of so-called 'effeminate' speech, which he believes includes broader than normal pitch range, sliding tonal effects between syllables, frequent use of dynamic pitch changes and occasional switches to falsetto voice. Lakoff (1975, 1977), whose assertions about female-typical stylistic features are at the centre of the debate and research outlined in chapter 7, claims that women are more likely than men to use deferential and inquisitive intonation, and says that women 'speak in italics' (Lakoff, 1975: 102). McConnell-Ginet (1978a) argues that women's higher pitch and more variable intonation are among the most important sources of the belief that women are emotional and unsuited to positions of societal responsibility.

Terrango (1966) studied the acoustical characteristics of 14 male voices, half of which were rated as very effeminate and half as very masculine (listener-judges were 117 women and 27 men). Only two of eight acoustical measures distinguished effeminate from masculine voices: the mean f_0 of the masculine voices (100 Hz) was lower than the normative figure for unselected American males (about 127 Hz while reading), although the mean for the effeminate voices (127 Hz) was not higher than average; and those speakers characterized as effeminate had steeper pitch shift gradients than the masculine speakers, whose average gradient was similar to the average American male's. Intonational dynamism is clearly associated with judgements of femininity, at least in the United States, while low pitch seems to be an important index of stereotypical masculinity.

The limited empirical evidence on women's and men's intonational usage suggests that there are some systematic differences between the sexes. First, women typically use a much wider range of pitch (f_0) in speaking than men do. Takefuta, Jancosek and Brunt (1971) recorded 12 men and 12 women speaking ten sentences, under instructions to use as many different intonations as they could think of. Acoustical measures of these recordings revealed that the standard deviation of the women's f_0 from the female mean was twice that of the men from their mean. Moreover, women's pitch shifts had a much sharper gradient over time than men's, indicating greater intonational dynamism.

Brend (1975) has reported on informal observations which indicate that female speakers use a 'polite' pattern of assertive intonation (e.g. 'Yés, yés/ Í knòw'), while men use a more 'deliberate' pattern (e.g. 'Yes yes/I knọw'), and further that women use certain patterns that men usually do not, notably 'surprise' patterns of high fall–rises, and others. She hypothesizes that men hardly ever use the highest contrastive tone level that women use, and that women therefore have a more varied range of tone changes to draw upon. McConnell-Ginet (1978a) reviews other evidence, which confirms both the greater pitch range and intonational variability of white middle-class women, in the United States at any rate.

In England, Pellowe and Jones (1978) report on data from their survey of Tyneside speech, in which men display a larger proportion of falling tones than rising tones, while women generally realize more rising tones. Elyan's (1978) analysis of 20 female and 20 male sudents in Bristol confirms these results, except that women here tended to use a more equal proportion of falls and rises, and hence displayed greater variability.

In English, intonational dynamism is expressed in recurrent patterns, such as those described above as 'polite' and 'deliberate'. Various systems have been developed that distinguish among a few basic 'tones', combinations of which can be superimposed on the transcript of an utterance to indicate the 'melody' or 'tune' that it follows (Crystal, 1975; Ladd, 1978, cited in McConnell-Ginet, 1978b; Gumperz, 1982; Brazil, 1978). It has been argued that each tone, and frequently encountered combinations of basic tones, carries emotional significance (or illocutionary force: Austin, 1962) that is widely recognized by people who share the same cultural background.

To date, however, one has had to rely on the insightful observations and intuitions of sociolinguists and anthropological linguists for hypotheses about these connotations. Research is now being conducted in order to substantiate the validity of these observations in controlled settings.

McConnell-Ginet (1978b), for example, discusses some pilot data from an interesting 'matched-guise' experiment. In this paradigm (Lambert, 1967; Giles and Powesland, 1975) the same voice is heard in different 'guises', representing different levels of the speech variables under investigation. These critical stimuli are typically interspersed among several distractor voices, designed to prevent listener-judges from becoming aware of hearing the same speaker more than once. This technique allows for some control over idiosyncratic differences between speakers that might otherwise be confounded with the speech variables of interest. In McConnell-Ginet's study, five different females and five males were recorded responding to the question, 'When will dinner be ready?' in each of two intonation patterns: the 'neural-fall' tone and the 'high-rise'. The high-rise 'six o'clóck' is the typical question tone that is stereotypically held to characterize women's responses to direct queries, while the neutral-fall 'six o'clock' typifies an assertive completion to the question–answer sequence. Listeners were asked to rate each of the 20 stimulus voices, interspersed among 12 distractors, on 16 personality scales.

The high-rise intonation was rated as reliably more hesitant, sympathetic, emotional and sociable than the neutral-fall, regardless of speaker sex. The neutral-fall was less evocative of strong associations with any personality traits, but was reliably more aggressive, decisive, assertive and dominant – again, whether spoken by women or by men. These two clusters of traits very nearly epitomize, respectively, stereotypical femininity and stereotypical masculinity as data in chapter 5 will show. It is significant that different intonation patterns elicited these attributions for speakers of both sexes, since it demonstrates that the mere recognition of a speaker's sex does not preclude a reassessment of his or her masculinity and femininity on the basis of subsequent speech.

Interestingly, in this pilot study ratings of the speakers on the individual items, masculine and feminine, were tied only modestly to differences in intonation, and only for female speakers, who were rated as sounding more masculine when using the falling tone and more feminine when speaking with the high-rise tone. However, the masculine and feminine items on a questionnaire are only two elements of a complex and far-reaching system of beliefs about men and women. When masculinity and femininity are referred to in this book it is in reference to this complex, and not to its individual components, two of which are potentially the items 'masculine' and 'feminine'. It is even conceivable that, in a climate of rapidly changing relations between the sexes, some people no longer consider women and men to differ on these items; i.e. they are no longer part of the sex stereotypes. But the same people may still consider that women and men are very different in other ways. In the McConnell-Ginet study, intonation was a fairly strong determinant of attributions of femininity and masculinity, although it was not a very good predictor of ratings on the feminine and masculine items.

While intonational dynamism and patterning are potent determinants of listeners' attributions no one has investigated how accurately these attributions reflect speakers' assessments of their own gender identity.

Paralinguistic correlates of perceived masculinity and femininity

Key (1975) provides an interesting synopsis of cross-cultural anthropological data on sex-associated paralinguistic variables, including the curious Mazateco 'whistle speech', which is articulated more or less exclusively by the men of this Mexican community. This apparently sophisticated paralinguistic system, based on whistles of varying pitch and duration, is capable of handling complex messages, and women rarely admit to being able to comprehend it. On a more mundane note, women in Sweden may express apparent agreement by articulating 'ja' with an intake of breath, while men do not.

According to the intuitions of North American media moguls, toughness and masculinity are signalled by low pitch and/or nasality (e.g. James Cagney, Humphrey Bogart and Clint Eastwood, to name but a few), while femininity is expressed in high, oral giggling sounds (e.g. Marilyn Monroe, Diane Keaton).

Two studies of the perceived personality correlates of vocal characteristics in adult women and men provide indirect support for the generality of these stereotypes. Addington (1968) recorded two women and two men who were trained to read a short passage again and again, each time simulating one of seven vocal qualities (breathy, thin, flat, nasal, tense, throaty, orotund) and one of three speech rates (slow, normal, fast), and pitch varieties (less variety than normal, normal, more variety than normal). Groups of trained judges then rated each voice sample for the presence or absence of the vocal parameters they were meant to exemplify, and 144 of the 252 samples were retained as adequate portrayals. Approximately 320 undergraduates each rated some of these 144 samples on 40 bipolar seven-point rating scales describing personality traits.

Analyses of variance revealed that, although women and men judges did not differ in their ratings of different voice samples, changes in male speakers' voices were rated differently from similar changes in female speakers' voices. The relationship between changes in speech and perceived personality was assessed by means of correlation, and quite different patterns of intercorrelations emerged for male and female speakers. Of the 23 personality scales for which correlations with speech variables were made (17 of the original 40 items were deleted from this analysis for various reasons), six were clearly related to contemporary feminine and masculine stereotypes (viz., masculine–feminine, kind–cruel, artistic–unartistic, sensitive–insensitive, talkative–quiet and enthusiastic–unenthusiastic).

Examination of the table of correlations for male speakers reveals that flatness in the voice correlates significantly with ratings towards the masculine pole of these six scales, and pitch variability correlates with feminine attributions. For female speakers, the pattern is more complex, but breathiness and thinness correlate with perceived masculinity.

Aronovitch (1976) had 100 students each rate half the samples of spontaneous speech recorded from 25 men and 32 women, on 10 scales similar to those used by Addington (1968). He also measured six objective parameters of each voice, including speech rate, sound/silence ratio, average intensity and intensity variance and average f_0 and f_0 variance. There were no differences between the personality ratings given by male and female listeners, but, as in Addington (1968), the pattern of intercorrelations between vocal parameters and personality ratings depended on the sex of the speaker.

Six of the 10 personality scales that were used for judging the speakers are unambiguously relevant to sex stereotypes. These are listed below, and the stereotypically masculine and feminine pole of each bipolar scale is designated by (M) and (F), respectively.

    1 Self-doubting (F)–Self-confident (M)
    2 Extraverted (M)–Introverted (F)
    3 Kind (F)–Cruel (M)
    4 Bold (M)–Cautious (F)
    5 Submissive (F)–Dominant (M)
    6 Emotional (F)–Unemotional (M)

The remaining four scales are either sex-stereotypically ambiguous or irrelevant (i.e. lazy–energetic; sociable–unsociable; humorous–serious; mature–immature).

Table 4.10   The direction of correlation between judgements on each of the six masculinity/femininity related personality items and the six vocal parameters measured by Aronovitch (1976)

	Rating scale											
	Male speakers						*Female speakers*					
Vocal measure	1	2	3	4	5	6	1	2	3	4	5	6
Intensity average	ns*	ns	ns	ns	ns	ns	M	M	ns	M	M	ns
Intensity variation	M	M	M	M	M	ns	ns	ns	F	ns	ns	F
f_0 average	ns	ns	ns	ns	ns	ns	ns	ns	ns	ns	ns	ns
f_0 variation	M	M	ns	M	M	ns	ns	ns	ns	ns	ns	ns
Speech rate	M	ns	ns	F	ns	ns	M	M	ns	M	M	M
Sound/silence	ns	ns	ns	ns	ns	ns	M	M	ns	M	M	ns

* ns = non-significant.

Table 4.1 is a tabulation, for each of the six vocal parameters, of the direction of correlation, in terms of perceived masculinity (M) or femininity (F), for each of the six sex-stereotypical scales listed above.

Apparently, judgements about male speakers on masculinity- and femininity-related scales were based on intensity of dynamism and pitch dynamism, while similar judgements for female speakers were based on the absolute intensity of their voices and the rate and fluency with which they spoke. In this study, less monotonous men were perceived as being more masculine, in contrast to the Addington (1968) study, where 'flatness' of speech was associated with masculinity. The correlations also indicate that women who spoke relatively slowly, quietly, disfluently and with higher voices were perceived to be more feminine. Comparisons with Addington's results on breathiness and throatiness in women are difficult to make, since it is not clear exactly what vocal parameters underlie Addington's variables.

Neither of these studies tackles the issue of sex-stereotypical speech directly; the authors were more concerned to discover whether the same standards are applied to both women and men in assessing personality from speech. However, the studies in this and the previous section are useful in suggesting a general approach to the discovery of sex-stereotypical speech features, by examining correlations between variations in judgement and variations in speech. Neither the Addington (1968) nor the Aronovitch (1976) study is a particularly good example of this approach, since in neither case is the choice of independent speech variables guided by explicit hypotheses, in terms of which the significance of the observed correlations can be interpreted. Furthermore, even a theory-guided orientation and rigorous operational procedures cannot circumvent the possibility that the *a priori* linguistic units observed or manipulated by the experimenter correspond only roughly, or not at all, to the variables actually influencing variations in subjects' responses. This is a problem endemic to all studies, such as most of those discussed in this chapter, that aim to control units of linguistic analysis that share a common label only by professional convention (i.e. formal linguistic units of analysis) and not because they are necessarily subjectively or functionally equivalent. The very least that is demanded in the face of such a plethora of particularistic and formalistic data as does exist is an attempt to reconstruct the whole that originally inspired analysis, by bringing together various strands of research on its constituents. It will be helpful to remember, however, that, despite esoteric experimental procedures and labyrinthine analytical categories, it is mundane human interaction that fuels professional interest in speech-based social judgement, and that it is people, not isolated speech variables, that are typically the objects of these judgements.

This suggests that it would be an altogether more efficient procedure to search for the people whose unadulterated speech produces judgements germane to the topic of interest (masculinity and femininity in this case) prior to searching for the linguistic parameters underlying these judgements. This suggestion will be taken up in earnest in chapter 6. But first it is necessary to review the other strands of piecemeal research that bear on speech-based judgements of masculinity and femininity.

Phonological and Grammatical Sex Differences: Clues to Masculine and Feminine Speech?

From studies concerning variables that are not determined by or defined in terms of units of pronunciation or grammar (referred to collectively as 'non-segmental'), attention is turned to studies of variables that are so defined (i.e. segmental variables). The most basic units of segmental analysis are the set of sounds, called 'phonemes', that are recognized as meaningfully distinct and non-interchangeable by the speakers of a language. These units comprise a complex *phonological system,* whose elements may be drawn upon both singly and in combination to produce the units of referential meaning that speakers of Indo-European languages know as words. Words and parts of words are pronounced in a great variety of different ways without altering the interpretation that is placed upon them, although these variations may have considerable implications for the light in which speakers are seen by others.

Strings of phonemes are also the subject of social conventions about how utterances should be constructed in order to convey information that cannot be conveyed by unorganized collections of words alone. The more stable of these conventions have been codified in what we know as 'grammars', which purport to represent the rules of combination that speakers need to know in order to be judged linguistically competent. As for pronunciation, however, deviation from convention is common, and does not necessarily disrupt the referential import of an utterance even though it may bear on how speakers are judged by others.

Phonology

Let us recall Labov's (1966) study of the pronunciation of English in New York City. The clearest difference between women and men was on the variable /th/ (as in *th*ing), where women more often produced the standard, or rhetorically correct, pronunciation (an interdental fricative, θ), while men often replaced the interdental fricative with another sound, often a stop consonant, like /t/ (as in *t*in), a usage that is generally recognized as socially disadvantageous, or stigmatized. This pattern was repeated, although less clearly, for the variable /dh/ (as in *th*ese and bro*th*er), for which men substituted the stop /d/ (as in *d*en) relatively more frequently, especially among speakers of lower SES.

There were no sex differences, on average, in the pronunciation of two vowel sounds, /eh/ (as in b*a*d), b*a*g) and /oh/ as in t*a*lk, d*o*g). However, examination of these variables in formal and informal contexts showed that women, especially so-called 'middle-class' women, produced at least as much, if not more, non-standard pronunciation as men in the informal part of the interview, but much less non-standard speech in the formal part. Labov termed this accentuated pattern of context-associated phonological variation 'hypercorrection'.

Since Labov's pioneering efforts, there have been dozens of similar studies which appear to support the conclusion that women's speech is on average closer to the norm of correct, standard behaviour than men's, especially in formal situations.

For example, in Montreal, Canada, Sankoff and Cedergren (1971) found that French Canadian women pronounced the liquid /l/ in pronouns and articles such as *il, elle, la,* and *les* more often than men. Romaine and Reid (1976) found that, among a group of Scottish schoolchildren, girls pronounced the dental /t/ in the middle and at the end of words (e.g. wa*t*er, go*t*) about 10 per cent more frequently than did boys, who more often replaced the dental with a glottal stop (*wa'er, go'*). In the United States women pronounce the post-vocalic /r/ in words like *car* and *bare*, which is the standard variant, more often than men do (Anshen, 1969; Labov, 1963; Levine and Crockett, 1966; Wolfram, 1969).

Fischer (1958), in the early study of children in a New England village, demonstrated that girls pronounced the standard progressive verb ending /-ing/ more frequently than boys, who realize /-in/ more often. Later studies of adults, both black and white speakers in the United States (Anshen, 1968; Fasold, 1968; Shuy, Wolfram and Riley, 1967; Wolfram, 1969) and white speakers in Norwich, England (Trudgill, 1975) have corroborated this tendency. In the same vein, studies in the United States (Anshen, 1969; Wolfram, 1969) and in Northern Ireland (Milroy, 1980), have confirmed Labov's (1966; also 1972) finding that men alter the interdental voiced fricative /th/ more frequently that women do.

With respect to vowel sounds, the standard pattern for women is repeated for the vowels studied in Detroit (Fasold, 1968; Shuy, Wolfram and Riley, 1967), London, England (Hudson and Holloway, 1977), Belfast (Milroy, 1980) and Glasgow (Macauley, 1978), and among English-speaking South Africans (Lanham and Macdonald, 1977), especially in formal contexts. The so-called hypercorrective pattern, involving accentuated shifts from non-standard to standard speech between informal and formal contexts, has also been manifest for women in Detroit on two vowels studied there (Fasold, 1968; Shuy, Wolfram and Riley, 1967).

Grammar

Sex differences in patterns of grammatical combination have not been found frequently. Wolfram (1969) found that men, especially from lower SES backgrounds, more often than women, reduced or omitted final consonant clusters that serve grammatical functions. For example, men deleted the final /-z/ from verbs in contexts where it indicates the third person singular (e.g. she *goes*, becomes, she *go*) 74 per cent of the time, and women only 68 per cent. Similar, but less regular, /-s/ deletion was found for the possessive form of nouns and pronouns and for plurals, where there was an average sex difference of about 5 per cent.

An interesting contrast to this picture is provided by Cheshire's (1978) study of the non-standard *addition* of an /-s/ suffix to the first and second person singular, and third person plural verb forms among adolescents in Reading, England. Here again, boys used the non-standard forms more frequently, sometimes by a margin of 50 per cent or more. In their study of Detroit English, Shuy, Wolfram and Riley (1976) found that men produced multiple negations (e.g. *We don't have no time*) 30 per cent more frequently than women in conversational speech (cf. also Wolfram, 1969; Wolfram and Fasold, 1974).

The data described in summary above would seem to warrant the apparently innocuous conclusion, drawn almost unanimously among investigators in the area, that women tend to be more standard speakers than men. This has tempted at least two authors (Haas, 1979; Lakoff, 1977) to include the relatively frequent use of standard speech as a component of feminine speech, and will probably tempt a more general enquiry into the masculine and feminine connotations of standard and non-standard speech variables.

However, the generalization about the relative use of standard features by women and men is premature in several ways, and these should be discussed in order to pre-empt the misguided expense of time and resources that the aforementioned endeavour would entail.

Methodological issues

The first point is that the differences that have been found are subtle and few, compared with the potentially unlimited opportunity for phonological and grammatical variation. The authors of recent urban linguistic surveys have been careful to point out that the speech variables they are interested in are usually better predicted by SES, ethnicity and age than by sex (e.g. Labov, 1970). Indeed, differences have sometimes not been found where expected. Labov (1966), for example, did not discover much difference betwen men and women in their pronunciation of post vocalic /-r/, or of /-ing/ in his New York study. Fasold (1972), in a study of tense-marking among black speakers in the United States, reports a similar absence of sex differences for several grammatical forms that distinguish standard from non-standard usage.

These considerations notwithstanding, to the extent that the differences that have been found are recurrent and consistent, even if only on a probabilistic basis, the generalization about sex-based phonological and grammatical differences is warranted. However, the relative proportion of women and men who use standard features has been shown above to vary from situation to situation, and while sociolinguists have generally been very sensitive to the causal role of context upon speech, they have almost universally failed in recent studies to consider the effects of one obvious source of contextual variation – the characteristics (sex, age, perceived status, etc.) of the interviewer. A dramatic, if exotic, illustration of the way in which interviewer sex, for example, could be important is provided by the Dravidian language of Kŭṛux, where only women pronounce the conjugation of verbs for the feminine gender, and then only when speaking with other women (Ekka, 1972; other examples are given in Bodine, 1975). Most of the early dialect interviews were conducted by male interviewers as far as can be determined (Anshen, 1969; Fasold, 1972; Fischer, 1958; Labov, 1963, 1966; Levine and Crockett, 1966; Macauley, 1978; Shuy, Wolfram and Riley, 1967; Trudgill, see below, 1975; Wolfram, 1969). Several surveys have now been carried out by women (e.g. Chesire, see below, 1978; Milroy, 1980; Sankoff and Cedergren, 1971) or possibly by women and men (e.g. Hudson and Holloway, 1977; Lanham and Macdonald, 1977; Romaine and Reid, 1976). However, the populations under study, the methods of interview and the linguistic variables of interest generally do not overlap in these different studies, and the influence of interviewer sex (and other interviewer characteristics) on sex differences in phonology and grammar thus remains of unknown quality and quantity.

Sociolinguists must, by virtue of the immense cost of analysing phonological data, be very selective in their choice of linguistic variables. Generally speaking, this choice is based on the intuition of insightful observers, who may themselves be speakers of the varieties in question. This reliance on intuition increases the risk that the selection will be biased in favour of stereotypical linguistic indicators. Less obvious variables, perhaps distributed in quite different ways, go undetected. This selective bias could have serious consequences for conclusions about sex-differentiated usage, since the differences are generally small, and less consistent than differences predicted by other social variables. A more complete picture of less obvious prestige-related variables derived from population-based research is called for.

The difficulties raised by these considerations are by no means insuperable, and one must suppose for the moment that appropriate interpretative and methodological refinements would not entirely undermine the generality of conclusions about male–female phonological and grammatical differences. Even so, to describe these differences in terms of 'prestige' and 'standard' speech is to make largely untested assumptions about the social significance of speech variables. A few of the more misleading assumptions are discussed below.

Problems with concepts of standard and prestige speech

The sociolinguistic concept of standard speech pertains almost exclusively to the domain of relative SES. The term *standard* is used interchangeably with *prestige*, or with the value of a way of speaking for upward social mobility (e.g. Weinreich, 1963). In so far as one is concerned to describe the distribution of prestige-related speech variables, the conclusion about women's more standard speech seems at first unproblematic.

However, it is evident that the context of relative prestige is only one of a variety of domains in which the idea of appropriate and acceptable, or standard, speech has applicability. In fact, it seems obvious that most interactions are pertinent to a variety of concerns and purposes at once, each of which has its own standards of normative behaviour. A systematic investigation of the dynamics of context-related ' norms has never been undertaken, but it is probable that behaviour that is standard *vis-à-vis* one normative domain may not be so in relation to another. There is little reason to suspect that prestige-related norms are very salient in either the typical sociolinguistic interview or in other speech elicitation situations, and hence the description of results in terms of prestige does not seem apt.

Traditional sociolinguistic procedure reflects a casual and rather naive attitude to the complexities of social analysis (cf. Smith, Giles and Hewstone, 1980; 1983), an attitude that is manifest again in the assumption that prestige norms are explicit and invariant, no matter who is speaking and who is listening. This assumption is implicit in the practice of codifying the standard variety prior to doing research on variation, and underpins the generalization that women use more prestige variants than men. One must, of course, have an objective standard against which to assess the magnitude and direction of individual variation, but care should be taken to ensure that this metric reflects the norms of the population to which it is attributed. Sociolinguistic practice does not have a built-in self-corrective mechanism which enables untested assumptions about the invariance of speech-related norms to be brought into line with social reality. Thus it begs the very question of how speech acquires its social and evaluative connotations, a question that is presumably at the heart of professional interest in sociolinguistic variation.

Given the fact that men and women typically occupy quite different social niches, and are often clearly differentiated even in those that they share, it would not be surprising to find that the sexes are habituated to different sets of context-dependent speech norms, and that their speech, and their impressions of others' speech, reflect these differences (cf. Thorne and Henley, 1975).

The assumption that the same prestige-related speech norms are attributable to female and male listeners, and apply equally to female and male speakers, must be put to the test before concluding that women use more standard speech. Very few

studies contain data relevant to this assumption, but those that do
suggest that it is unfounded. This is illustrated below.

Empirical evidence for the non-uniformity of prestige and standard speech norms

In Labov's (1966) New York study, speakers' perceptions of the
prestige norm, and their evaluative reactions to non-prestige
speech, were elicited by means of three tests. In the Subjective
Reaction Test, participants heard 22 sentences taken from
interviews with five individual women, chosen to represent
different values of the five phonological variables of interest. For
each sentence, the participants had to choose, from among a
range of jobs that varied along a prestige continuum from 'factory
worker' to 'television personality', the probable occupation of the
speaker. While SES, ethnicity and age were better predictors of
participants' judgements than was sex, women were slightly more
sensitive to /oh/ variation, and men were clearly more sensitive to
/th/ and /dh/ variation. That is, men made slightly more and
women slightly less homogeneous judgements for different
varieties of /oh/, while the opposite pattern was found for /th/
and /dh/.

In the second test, the Self-evaluative Test, participants heard
the interviewer, a trained phonetician, read each of a list of words
in several different ways, again representing different levels of
the five phonological variables. For each word, the participants
chose the pronunciation alternative that they believed to be most
characteristic of their own speech. Both men and women
reported that they used more of the prestige variants than they
were actually observed to do, and no sex differences in the rate of
over-reporting are mentioned.

On the third test, the participants had to indicate, for 18
words, (1) which of two pronunciations was more 'correct', and
(2) which of the two they actually used. Labov reasoned
that the discrepancy between (1) and (2) would be a good
measure of a participant's manifest insecurity about his/her
own speech, and called this the Index of Linguistic Insecurity
(ISI). Men had an average ISI score of 2.1, and women 3.6,
out of a possible 18, although, because of the nature of the score,

one cannot tell if this was due to sex differences on part (1) or part (2), or both.

On two out of three tests, the women and men in Labov's study differed in their reactions to speech supposedly representative of general prestige norms. Parenthetically, even greater differences were predicted by SES and ethnicity. Clearly, normative standards in this study were not uniform, and do not warrant the assumption underlying the conclusion about women's more prestigious speech.

Similar results are reported by Trudgill (1975), who found that the men in his study of Norwich English reported that they used more of the supposedly non-standard variants of several vowels than they were actually observed to do, while women continued on average to over-report their use of 'prestige' variants. The norms of men and women differed in certain fundamental respects in this work, and Trudgill chose the term 'covert prestige' to characterize the men's unexpected rejection of the assumed prestige norms, and their adoption of another. Trudgill's results themselves would seem to indicate that these alternative norms are not all that covert, however, and the choice of terms is tantamount to admitting that the sociolinguist's assumptions are in need of recalibration.

The fact that prestige-related norms are not uniform with the sociolinguistic concept of standard speech, at least with respect to the variables that have been studied, indicates that it would be wise to abandon the tempting plan to investigate the feminine and masculine connotations of standard and non-standard speech. As a retrospective critique, the foregoing discussion will hopefully encourage the re-evaluation of some seemingly unambiguous data and research procedures. On a more positive note, the idea that speech-related norms are dynamic and multifaceted is consistent with the more general idea that beliefs and expectations are context- and participant-dependent in ways that empirical enquiry can help to clarify. More specifically to the topic of this chapter, one is concerned to discover the context- and participant-related standards of masculine and feminine speech. It is regrettable that the conceptual framework in terms of which the apparent sex differences have been described above cannot be of more help as a starting point in this endeavour.

Social Psychological Studies of Masculine and Feminine Attribution to Speakers with Different Regional Accents

Finally, I shall examine the results of several exploratory studies from experimental social psychology, where speakers with different regional accents have been judged on traits relevant to masculinity and femininity. These studies (reviewed in Giles *et al.*, 1980) were originally inspired by the consistent finding that speakers of 'standard' British English, or 'received pronunciation' (RP, also widely known as BBC English), are rated differently from local and regional accented speakers in matched-guise experiments. RP speakers are regularly upgraded on competence and status-related traits to non-RP speakers, who are usually perceived as more socially attractive and trustworthy (see Giles and Powesland, 1975, for a review). However, most of these results were obtained from studies using only male stimulus voices. Prior to 1978, the only exception to this was a matched-guise study by Cheyne (1970), wherein Scottish and English listeners' reactions to Scottish and English accented speakers (two female and two male) were compared. English accented speakers (RP accented, one assumes), irrespective of sex, were perceived to be more socially competent (e.g. prestigious, intelligent and ambitious), and Scottish speakers to be slightly more sociable. However, this differentiation was much clearer for the male stimulus voices; perceived differences between female speakers were less pervasive and less accentuated.

Elyan *et al.* (1978) attempted to extend the results based on female speakers and asked 76 listeners to judge female RP and Lancashire accented speakers on traits related to competence and social attractiveness, stereotypical femininity and masculinity, and the speakers' attitudes towards male–female relations. The results confirmed the general finding that RP speakers are perceived as more competent and less unattractive than regional speakers. However, additional and unexpected findings emerged. Female RP speakers were rated significantly higher on masculine stereotypical items (adventurous, independent, aggressive and egotistic) and at the same time higher on the feminine item and on items related to egalitarian sex-role beliefs. These surprising results were tentatively interpreted as showing that female RP speakers are perceived to personify elements of both femininity and masculinity; that is, they were seen to represent 'psychological androgyny' (see chapter 5).

Follow-up work was obviously needed to validate these findings and to extend their generality. An especially urgent priority was to discover the perceived femininity and masculinity of male RP and regional speakers. Giles and Marsh (1979) recorded two male and two female bidialectal (RP and south Welsh) speakers reading a short prose passage in their two different guises. Another 76 women and men (half of each sex) rated these speakers on items taken from Elyan et al. (1978). RP speakers, irrespective of sex, were rated as more competent, egalitarian and masculine (i.e. independent and egotistic). At the same time, female RP speakers were rated as no less feminine than south Welsh accented speakers. Female speakers were rated as more feminine, less masculine and less competent than male speakers, irrespective of accent guise.

These results were interpreted as supporting the conclusion that female RP speech tends to be seen as the personification of psychological androgyny relative to male RP and regional guises, and to female regional guises, at least as far as the exploratory nature of these studies would permit any such generalizations. Giles et al. (1980), however, argued that the apparently femininity- and masculinity-related results of Elyan et al. (1978) and Giles and Marsh (1979) were artifactual, as a consequence of a biased selection of masculinity and femininity items on the questionnaires. They demonstrated that two of the so-called masculine-stereotypical items on which RP women in the Elyan et al. (1978) were rated higher (adventurous and egotistical) are also middle-class (as opposed to working-class) stereotypical. Thus, the fact that RP accented women were upgraded on these items relative to regional accented women may have had more to do with the congruity between the SES-related connotations of RP speech and these items than with the masculine connotations of the items. It remains true that RP women were also rated higher on aggression, a stereotypically masculine and working-class trait, and on independence, a masculine trait free of SES-related connotations; but the basis for the conclusion about androgynously perceived RP women is considerably weakened. Similarly, the apparently masculine connotations of female RP speech found by Giles and Marsh (1979) were based on two items, one of which (egotistical) is middle-class and masculine, leaving only the item 'independence' as an unequivocal basis for the conclusion about the androgynous RP accented females.

The importance of the Giles *et al.* (1980) contribution lies in the suggestion that the significance attached to speech varieties by researchers, even when informed by the response of many listeners, may be at variance with the interpretations actually underlying listeners' responses. Furthermore, they are able to demonstrate the utility of a procedure designed to correct for this interpretative discrepancy. Having shown that many trait-descriptive terms are at one and the same time stereotypically sex-associated and SES-associated, they selected a pool of items made up of equal proportions of middle-class and working-class masculine and feminine traits (three items from each of the four categories). Listeners (30 male and 30 female) were asked to rate the personalities of a male and female speaker, each speaking in two guises (RP and Yorkshire accents), on these 12 items, plus another eight items selected for their clearly sex-stereotypical and SES-non-stereotypical connotations.

The results of this study supported the argument of Giles *et al.* RP speakers, irrespective of sex, were rated higher on middle-class items with both masculine and feminine overtones; Yorkshire speakers were rated higher on working-class items. Male speakers received higher ratings on masculine items irrespective of their SES connotations, and female speakers were rated higher on feminine items. There were no indications that any one speaker was perceived in more androgynous terms than the next.

It must be emphasized at this point that these results, and their implications for the interpretations of the Elyan *et al.* (1978) and Giles and Marsh (1979) studies, do not disconfirm the hypothesis that accent varieties in England and elsewhere carry clear masculine and feminine connotations in relation to one another. None of the aforementioned studies explicitly set out to test such an hypothesis, nor did they compare a wide variety of accent types on a broad range of items chosen explicitly and only for their relevance to sex stereotypes. Rather, they pertain to the rather particular hypothesis, seemingly disconfirmed, that female RP speakers are perceived in androgynous terms. The more general question about the relationship between accentedness and perceived femininity and masculinity has yet to come under empirical scrutiny.

The social psychological approach to discovering the social significance of speech style exemplified by the studies described in the penultimate section of this chapter, and aspects of which have been employed by Labov and Trudgill, potentially avoid some of the more lethal assumptions about the meaning of speech variables and the prevalence of context-dependent norms. Another advantage of these studies is that they employ relatively lengthy examples of ordinary speech as stimuli to social judgement. However, there is no doubt that a degree of linguistic control is sacrificed in the matched-guise paradigm, and that the varieties produced by bi-dialectal speakers may be based on stereotypes in the same way as those that guide intuitive choices of isolated, 'representative' speech variables. Furthermore, despite the fact that matched-guise speakers are instructed to keep emotional coloration and paralinguistic activity constant from guise to guise, there is little doubt that intonational and paralinguistic cues are among important components of regional accent varieties, and of stereotypes about them.

Social psychological and sociolinguistic skills could obviously be merged to mutual advantage in the endeavour to clarify what, if any, are the phonological and grammatical correlates of unambiguously masculine and feminine speech. To date, however, the particular preoccupations of each discipline have prevented such a marriage, even though it is essential that adherents of different approaches are eventually able to translate each other's descriptions if there is to be any hope of collaboration.

Conclusions

This concludes our review of the evidence for speech-based cues to the attribution of masculinity and femininity. Studies have shown that variations in vocal pitch, vocal tract resonance, intonational dynamism, vocal intensity, paralinguistic voice quality and possibly pronunciation and grammar are stereotypically sex-associated, and potentially evocative of reliable inferences about speakers' masculinity and femininity. Speech, it seems, is seen as a reliable basis for assessing the degree to which speakers conform to what is generally expected of their sex.

A relatively detailed analysis of the evidence was needed in order firmly to establish this point before proceeding to an investigation of how these attributions may be related to speakers' own masculine and feminine self-images, and to this facet of listeners' social identity.

It hardly needs to be stressed that we typically hear the speech variables discussed in the foregoing chapter in concert, in the situated speech of ordinary people going about their daily lives. Without wishing for a moment to denigrate the value of detailed analysis in the description of speech, it is clear that the potluck approach to the discovery of masculine and feminine speech typified by most of the sociolinguistic and anthropological studies described is very inefficient. Above and beyond the demanding preoccupation with sex differences, the widespread reliance on intuitive sensitivity as a method of selecting speech variables for empirical attention ensures that less obvious features of sex-stereotypical speech will be a long time finding their way into scholarly descriptions. The only alternative to intuition offered by contemporary sociolinguistics, which is in general concerned more with language than with the people who speak it, is trial-and-error sampling of one speech variable or combination of variables after another, *ad infinitum*. Surely it would be more fruitful to move from the global to the particular in the discovery and description of feminine and masculine speech, rather than trying to assemble a fragmented picture of the whole on the basis of informed guesses about its constituent parts.

To describe masculine and feminine speech is not, however, the singular aim of this chapter, beyond demonstrating that speech can stimulate reliable imputations of speakers' masculinity and femininity. In the studies to be described in chapter 6, listeners were asked to form impressions of speakers on the basis of undoctored speech samples recorded in a carefully controlled setting. As would be expected on the basis of the foregoing reviews, very reliable patterns of femininity and masculinity attribution were observed, and future resources could profitably be invested in the analysis and description of the linguistic antecedents of these differential responses.

The present concern, however, is to seek explanations for the observed patterns of response as a function of speakers' and listener-judges' self-assessed conformity to sex-stereotypical standards of demeanour and behaviour, and to examine the evaluative concomitants of these judgements.

Before returning to these issues in chapter 6, the procedures that have been developed to measure femininity and masculinity must be discussed with a view to critical appraisal and, eventually, revision. Chapter 5 begins with an overview of the history of the measurement of masculinity and femininity in psychology, and describes a study that is aimed at overcoming some of the more obvious problems of contemporary masculinity/ femininity measures; chapter 6 then describes the results of applying a new measurement technique to the questionnaire data introduced in chapter 5.

5

The Measurement of Femininity and Masculinity

It might seem quite a simple matter to obtain a measure of someone's femininity and masculinity, at least on the face of it. All that we require is some way of determining the degree to which people think that they conform to the characteristics typically associated with women and men, respectively. In fact, there are a number of questionnaires purporting to measure masculinity–femininity (MF), which differ widely in their aims, assumptions and methods. Overall, they fall into two groups, based on the methods used to build the questionnaires, and to score femininity and masculinity. These will be described below.

Instruments of the first kind, which I call 'sex difference' MF measures, are not compatible with the aim of assessing self-perceived masculinity and femininity as they are presently conceived. More recent developments, however, have led to the emergence of another approach, which in principle is compatible with this aim. The transition to the 'self-categorization' method, as it shall be called, has not been entirely clear-cut, nor is it yet complete. Still, as we shall see, the requirements for an approach to the measurement of masculinity and femininity that defines gender identity in terms of self-perceived conformity to sex-stereotypical standards of character and behaviour have almost been met by several popular instruments which will be briefly described later in the chapter. Finally, the results of a study of sex stereotypes and attitudes will be described as the basis for a more refined sex stereotype MF measure that overcomes some of the weaknesses in others.

The Sex Difference Method: Exemplars of the Paradigm

In a landmark review of MF measurement, Constantinople (1973) gave details of the test construction procedures that were used in developing the then five most widely used MF tests: the Terman–Miles MF Test (Terman and Miles, 1936); the MF Scale of the Strong Vocational Interest Blank (SVIB) (Strong, 1943); the Minnesota Multiphasic Personality Inventory (MMPI) MF Scale (Dahlstrom and Welsh, 1960); the California Psychological Inventory (CPI) Fe Scale (Gough, 1966); and the Inventory GAMIN M Factor (Guilford and Guilford, 1936).

The most interesting and earliest of these, the Terman–Miles MF Test, consists of seven exercises, ranging from a word-association task to an opinion questionnaire, each made up of several items. In developing the test, items that did not reliably distinguish between the responses of women and men were weeded out. In the final version of the test, masculine responses, i.e. those consistent with the way that most men have been shown to respond, are scored +1 and feminine responses are scored − 1. The test yields one overall MF score, which is simply the algebraic sum of the +'s and −'s scored on the individual items, with some weighting adjustments based on the reliability and overlap of the exercises.

Terman and Miles's (1936) procedures established a model for MF test construction that was copied, with minor variations, by the proponents of the other four tests named above. All but one of these instruments, which consist of responses to self-report questions (e.g. 'I would like to be a florist', or 'I am entirely self-confident'), included items that distinguished women from men and excluded items that did not. The one exception, the MMPI MF Scale, further excluded items that did not distinguish a group of homosexual and 'sexually inverted' males from a group of 'normal' males. The fourth test, the Inventory GAMIN M Factor, comprises items that distinguished between the highest and lowest-scoring quartiles on a factor that emerged initially from a factor analysis of an introversion–extraversion test. High loadings on the factor indicated positive responses to the items, 'is a male', 'not absent-minded', and 'more interested in athletics than intellectual things', among others that were masculine in tone. However, the criterion for including items on this test was not, strictly speaking, sex difference in response, since there were actually 16 women in the top quartile and 12 men in the bottom quartile, out of a total of 800 respondents. Regardless of the conceptual confusion behind such a measure, reliable sex differences in response in subsequent applications of the test are offered as testament to its validity, as they are for the other four tests.

Besides being based on a sex difference criterion for item inclusion and test validation, these instruments all yield a single composite MF score, usually based on the algebraic sum of responses to dichotomous true–false, plus–minus or yes–no items. Occasionally, there is a neutral response option, in which the respondent is not forced to choose between an endorsement and a denial, but these responses are not usually taken into consideration in totalling the final MF score.

Criticisms of the Sex Difference Method

Three major criticisms have been levelled at the approach to MF measurement exemplified by the instruments described above by Constantinople (1973) and others (e.g. Bem, 1974; Spence, Helmreich and Stapp, 1975; Worell, 1978). The first and, from a theoretical point of view, most damning is aimed at the adoption of a sex difference definition of MF. The rationale underlying the development of the sex difference MF tests was to differentiate men from women, and their efficiency has been judged mainly in terms of how well they do this (Constantinople, 1973). The clinical motive inspiring these developments (although it is extremely difficult to find clear statements pertaining to researchers' interests in MF) was presumably the desire for a diagnostic instrument that would identify those who deviate from sex-associated standards of behaviour, attitude, opinion, etc. This deviance was assumed to cause psychological problems for the individual or for others with whom they had contact. The assumption implicit in the sex difference MF tests, which has been shown in previous chapters to have little empirical support, is that current sex-associated standards of behaviour, attitude, etc. – in other words, *sex stereotypes* –simply reflect *sex differences* in behaviour, attitude, etc. While there is probably a causal interaction between sex differences and sex stereotypes, it is unlikely that this link is either one-way or direct.

In short, the premise that scores on a sex difference MF test will predict either attributions of conformity to sex stereotypes or masculinity and femininity self-images is unsubstantiated. Furthermore, if one takes the sex difference criterion at its word, then the extent to which men ever score high on femininity on a test and women ever score high on masculinity can be taken as a precise estimate of that test's inefficiency. As the sex difference diagnostic criterion becomes more efficiently operationalized and applied, femininity and masculinity are defined out of existence, and one is left with what one had in the first place, namely women and men. There are better ways of telling the sexes apart.

The second major criticism of these tests is that femininity and masculinity are conceived of as two poles of a single continuum, tied to each other by the principle of reciprocal interdependence: whosoever is not feminine is by definition masculine. This inverse relationship has its conceptual foundation in the sex difference criterion, which entails that each item on the test, and the test overall, distinguishes as categorically and reliably as possible between women and men. It is consolidated operationally by two aspects of the scoring procedure. First, a response not scored as feminine is scored as masculine, and vice versa; each response has implications for both femininity and masculinity. Second, only one score, an MF score representing the sum of masculine minus feminine responses, or even just the number of feminine responses (on the CPI Fe Scale), is the basis for inferences about masculinity and femininity.

Many critics, especially the proponents of new MF measures reviewed below, have singled out implicit bipolarity as the single most serious shortcoming of these tests, since it does not permit the independent measurement of masculinity and femininity (e.g. Bem, 1974; Constantinople, 1973; Spence, Helmreich and Stapp, 1975). These researchers advocate the incorporation of operationally independent femininity and masculinity scales within MF tests, especially with a view to discovering the correlates, antecedents and implications of variations in either masculinity or femininity alone. This would also permit the measurement of *psychological androgyny* (Heilbrun, 1973; Bem, 1974), conceived of as the extent to which an individual combines elements of both masculinity and femininity gender identity, and *undifferentiated gender identity,* where individuals do not define themselves in either masculine or feminine terms (e.g. Spence, Helmreich and Stapp, 1975).

Bipolarity has been seen by these authors as a methodoligical problem that can be resolved by the administration of instruments with separate femininity and masculinity scales. Indeed, attempts have been made to increase the flexibility of sex difference MF tests by separating masculinity and femininity scales (Beaucom, 1976; Heilbrun, 1976). However, from the present point of view, bipolarity is methodologically consistent with the sex difference approach, which strives for perfect categorical (male–female) diagnosticity. The ideally feminine person would respond to all the items in a categorically female-like way, and the masculine person would respond in a male-like way. In so far as perfect diagnosticity is impossible to achieve, the most direct way of coping with response patterns that are ambiguous from the point of view of a female–male dichotomy is to extend the dichotomous classification into a bipolar continuum that ranges from ideal femininity to ideal masculinity. In this light, amendments to sex difference MF tests that unyoke masculinity from femininity (e.g. Beaucom, 1976; Heilbrun, 1976; 1981) positively undermine the theoretical aim of the approach. It is significant, and not just coincidental, that the chief protagonists of MF instruments with independent femininity and masculinity scales have *also abandoned the sex difference criterion.*

The third major criticism of the MF tests subsumed under the sex difference rubric is that none of these tests presents a profile of subscores on components of the overall score or uses a factorial approach to test development or validation. This is unfortunate, because several of the tests include items drawn from more than one source (Terman–Miles MF Test; MMPI MF Scale) or from sources whose homogeneity is not obvious (SVIB MF Scale; CPI Fe Scale; GAMIN M Factor).

Factor analytic studies of sex difference MF measures (notably Lunneborg and Lunneborg, 1970, and Lunneborg, 1972) have shown that there may be more than ten factors underlying people's responses to the various scales. The majority of these factors do not discriminate between the sexes as well as they should. Estimates of the proportion of the variance in response to these tests arising from sex differences range in the neighbourhood of 20 per cent (Constantinople, 1973). Lunneborg (1972) suggests that at least some of the presently unreliable items might at one time have differentiated men from women, but did so because of people's conformity to the then-popular sex stereotypes. As the stereotypes have changed, many of the original items have become obsolete.

The idea that sex stereotypes may play an active role, through socialization and normative pressure, in the development and manifestation of sex differences has been mooted at several points in this book, and is also topical in the area of MF research (e.g. Broverman, *et al.*, 1972; Sherman, 1976). While it seals the fate of the sex difference approach, it also leads to a way out of this logical and empirical cul-de-sac. Whether or not there is congruity between sex stereotypes and sex differences, it is sex stereotypes – the system of shared expectations about what women and men are like – and not sex differences *per se* that are relevant in everyday judgements about one's own, and other people's, femininity and masculinity.

Transition to the Self-categorization Method: Sex Differences and Sex Stereotypes

An instructive glimpse into the possible structure of the relationship between sex differences in response and stereotypes about sex differences is afforded by an innovative study of MF tests. Nichols (1962) administered a scale of 356 'true–false' items taken from sex difference type MF tests to men and women, and subjects rated themselves on each. On the basis of these ratings, he calculated the phi coefficient of each item's ability to discriminate between the sexes. He then administered the same scale to a new group of subjects, asking them to indicate for each item which response would be given more often by men and which by women. Phi coefficients were calculated for the extent to which each item was rated as if it were believed to discriminate between the sexes.

Nichols constructed a two-dimensional scatterplot, plotting each item according to the magnitude and sign of its two phi coefficients, representing its actual and stereotypical abililty to discriminate women from men. Items high on both actual and stereotypical discriminability he termed 'obvious' because of the isomorphic, and hence putatively obvious, link between sex differences and stereotypes that they represent. Of the 356 items, 58 were 'obvious', making it very plausible to imagine a causal link between sex stereotypes and responses on sex difference MF tests. More interestingly, responses to a further 60 items correlated significantly with stereotypical, but not with actual, discriminability, and 208 items did not reach significance for either stereotypical or actual discriminative power. As long ago as 1962, more than half the original items were already obsolete from the point of view of the aims of the tests on which they appear, even though one third of these survived in sex stereotypes. Finally, items that correlated with actual sex differences in response, but not with beliefs about sex differences, Nichols termed 'subtle'. There were only 30 such items. When compared with the 60 items for which stereotypes only are evident and the 50 items where sex differences are matched by stereotypes, it is clear that, in this context at least, stereotypes not only largely subsume sex differences, but exaggerate and elaborate upon them.

These results, and those of Lunneborg (1972; Lunneborg and Lunneborg, 1970), indicate that, ironically, sex difference MF tests are in fact better measures of conformity to sex stereotypes than they are of sex differences in response. Consequently, they may produce results that are empirically quite similar to those produced by sex stereotype MF instruments (e.g. Wiggins and Holzmuller, 1978). However, MF instruments that are not based explicitly on a sex stereotype criterion, or those in which femininity and masculinity are either operationalized or measured as if they are by definition reciprocally interdependent, are not suited to present aims.

Empirical Antecedents of the Self-categorization Method

An early example of a social consensus definition of MF, although it is not a sex stereotype definition, is provided by Jenkin and Vroegh (1969), who use these terms to 'denote the complexes of attributes which are generally considered appropriate and essential in a given society to the personalities of males and females, respectively' (p. 679). In addition, they argue that 'there are no more grounds for regarding masculinity as the opposite of femininity than there are for regarding male as the opposite of female' (p. 680), and therefore that masculinity and femininity are two separate dimensions, each applicable to only one sex (cf. also Vroegh, 1971).

The move towards a definition based on social consensus and the independence of masculinity and femininity are steps in the right direction, but Jenkin and Vroegh's (1969) conceptualization is still restrictive on three counts. First, although stereotype questionnaires are typically concerned with personality characteristics (presumably because these are amenable to paper and pencil measurement procedures), it is valid, and will eventually be essential, to enquire about sex stereotypes on any dimension that could conceivably differentiate women from men, including behaviours, skills, aspirations, emotional experiences, social roles, physical characteristics, material possessions and so on. In other words, the concept of a sex stereotype should capture the aggregate of ways in which men and women differ. Second, the concept of sex stereotype needs to be expanded to refer to attributes in addition to those that are considered appropriate and essential, attributes that are seen as inappropriate but tolerated, and non-essential but expected, concomitants of sex group membership (Stoppard and Kalin, 1978).

Finally, Jenkin and Vroegh's (1969) argument that femininity should apply only to women, and masculinity only to men, is misleading. They fail to distinguish between operationalizing sex stereotypes and using them as criteria for measuring gender identity. As far as deriving and charting the stereotypes go, femininity and masculinity are not opposites, as Jenkin and

Vroegh point out: they are comparative concepts whose essence lies in the fact that they epitomize the ways in which women and men are *believed* to be distinctive. Sex stereotypes have no *a priori* empirical referents or standards of external validity. There is no paradox in the idea that some men might see themselves in somewhat feminine terms, for example, since it is not women *per se,* but shared ideas *about* women, that are the arbiters of the concept of femininity.

A more direct antecedent of the self-categorization approach is to be found in research on the desirability of sex stereotypes carried out by Rosenkrantz *et al.* (1976). They had women and men rate 122 seven-point interval scales, labelled with descriptive adjectives such as 'emotional', 'direct', 'appreciates art and literature', three times for the concepts 'adult male', 'adult female' and 'self'. This procedure for eliciting sex stereotypes, allowing for a latitude of item endorsement (seven-point rating scales), and the independent operationalization of masculine and feminine stereotypes is a great improvement over dichotomous (e.g. true–false) or bipolar (male–female) procedures.

Rosenkrantz *et al.* (1968) grouped the items into clusters, based on the degree of consensus among the raters as to whether an item was more typical of an 'adult female' or an 'adult male'. On 41 items, there was greater than 75 per cent consensus among raters that the adjective was more typical of one sex than the other. A further 78 items significantly differentiated the stereotypes, but at a lower rate of consensus. Raters agreed that 24 items were no more typical of one sex than the other. Finally, male and female raters differed significantly in their attributions of 9 adjectives. These items were excluded from further analysis because they indicated an absence of consensus.

Rosenkrantz *et al.* (1968) could have presented data on the degree of match–mismatch between the sex stereotypes and the raters' self-concepts. Instead, they opted for an extension of the study designed to assess the social desirability of the respective stereotypes. They did this by asking a new group of raters simply to indicate which pole of each item was more socially desirable. This foray into the domain of social desirability was an interesting departure from the straightforward study of sex stereotypes, but it appears to have inspired practices that impose special limitations on sex stereotype MF measures, namely to include only socially desirable items in their operationalizations.

The Self-categorization Method: Exemplars of the Paradigm

The three widely cited MF tests that come closest to exemplifying the self-categorization approach (the Bem Sex Role Inventory (BSRI): Bem, 1974; the Personal Attributes Questionnaire (PAQ): Spence, Helmreich and Stapp, 1975; and the Personality Research Form (PRF ANDRO Scale). Berzins, Welling and Wetter, 1978) are all based on rather loose operationalizations of sex stereotypes, and, for reasons that are not made explicit, use only socially desirable adjectives on their scales.

Bem (1974) developed the BSRI primarily in order to distinguish highly sex-typed individuals from those who might be characterized by aspects of both femininity and masculinity, whom she labels psychologically 'androgynous'. She defines the sex-typed individual as 'someone who has internalized society's sex-typed standards of desirable behaviour for men and women' (1974: p. 155). The 20 masculine characteristics on the BSRI were chosen from among a number of characteristics that were rated by both women and men as significantly more desirable for 'an American man' than for 'an American woman', and vice versa for the 20 feminine items. Examples of items on the masculinity scale are *athletic, masculine* and *forceful;* while *cheerful, gentle* and *softspoken* are on the femininity scale. No reference is made in the operationalization of masculinity and femininity here to how typical the items are to either sex, but merely to how desirable they are. Because the items were initally culled from a large and loosely stereotypical pool, it is possible that they are stereotypical as well as desirable; but this is by no means necessarily so, for one can think of characteristics that one would like to see in other people, but that do not form part of our current beliefs about them.

Originally, individuals who were administered the BSRI were asked to indicate, on seven-point scales, how well each of the femininity and masculinity items characterize themselves, and their femininity and masculinity scores were calculated as the mean self-rating for all items on each scale. Bem (1974) also computed an androgyny score for each subject, defined as the student's t-ratio of the difference between a person's masculine and feminine self-assessment. This score reflects the relative amounts of femininity and masculinity that subjects include in their self-descriptions, so that someone scoring low on both masculinity and femininity receives the same androgyny score as someone scoring high on both scales. Strahan (1975), and Spence, Helmreich and Stapp (1975), criticized this scoring procedure on the basis of hypotheses about differences between high-masculinity–high-femininity scorers, for whom they retain the label 'androgynous' and low-masculinity–low-femininity scorers, whom they label 'undifferentiated'. Bem (1977) acknowledged this criticism, and herself adopted the quadripartite masculine–feminine–androgynous–undifferentiated distinction, whereby subjects are classified into one of the four gender identity categories depending upon the absolute level of both masculinity and femininity scores. A median split procedure is usually used to classify subjects into one of the four quadrants defined by the intersection of masculinity and femininity as illustrated in figure 5.1.

The PRF ANDRO Scale was designed 'to approximate the BSRI using items selected from a standardized personality test' (Kelly and Worell, 1977: 1104; cf. Berzins, Welling and Wetter, 1978), and thus it is not surprising that it operates with definitions very similar to Bem's. The investigators used their own intuition to select 29 supposedly stereotypical and socially desirable masculine items from among the 440 items that make up the Personality Research Form for inclusion on the ANDRO Scale.

The PAQ (Spence and Helmreich, 1980; Spence, Helmreich and Stapp, 1975) also confounds social desirability with stereotypes in its measure of masculinity and femininity. The PAQ consists of 55 items taken from an extended version of the Rosenkrantz *et al.* (1968) stereotype questionnaire, which were found to distinguish concept 'typical male college student' from the concept 'typical female college student' when rated by a university population. These 55 items were subsequently rated for the concepts 'ideal female' and 'ideal male' by a new sample of subjects whose ratings were taken as a measure of social

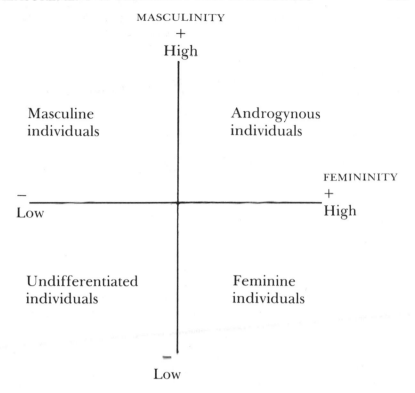

Figure 5.1 The representation of masculinity and femininity as independent and continuous dimensions of the self-image, intersecting to define the categories of Androgynous, Masculine, Feminine and Undifferentiated individuals

desirability. If the ratings for the 'ideal' female and male were both in the same direction, the item was called either 'female-valued' or 'male-valued', depending upon whether the favoured pole was congruent with the stereotypically female or male pole. If ratings for the 'ideal' male and female differed in direction, the item was called 'sex-specific'. There were 23 male-valued, 18 female-valued and 13 sex-specific items. Spence, Helmreich and Stapp (1975) argue that the male-valued and female-valued scales are conceptually most similar to Bem's (1974) masculinity and femininity scales, inasmuch as they include only sex-stereotypical, desirable items. Consistent with this, they present the results of women's and men's self and stereotype ratings, and their interrelationships, in terms of the male-valued, female-valued and sex-specific subscales of the PAQ, none of which is equivalent to an unconfounded stereotype.

Criticisms of these Masculinity/Femininity Measures

The BSRI, the PAQ and the PRF ANDRO Scale, which adopt definitions of masculinity and femininity that approximate sex stereotypes, and which both operationalize and measure masculinity and femininity independently, come close to satisfying the requirements of being able to assess the extent to which individuals see themselves in sex-stereotypical terms. However, preoccupation with the separate measurement of masculinity and femininity and psychological androgyny have meant that the transition to a social stereotype criterion of masculinity and femininity, upon which the success of the aforementioned innovations is contingent, is not quite complete.

In particular, three serious shortcomings of existing measures must be corrected in order to obtain a procedure that is satisfactory from the present point of view. Two of these shortcomings have already been alluded to. The first is that the masculinity and femininity criteria against which individuals' self-images are compared or scored (ie. the items that make up the masculinity and femininity scales) have been operationalized on the BSRI and on the PRF ANDRO Scale on the basis of very casual and unreliable stereotype elicitation methods (intuition, in the case of the PRF ANDRO Scale: see Myers and Gonda, 1982a,b). The integrity of the PAQ fares somewhat better in terms of its developmental history, being based on a reasonably rigorous study of sex stereotypes (Rosenkrantz et al., 1968).

The second shortcoming is that, on all the scales, the major prerequisite for an item to be included on the instrument is not sex stereotypicality but rather social desirability. There is no *a priori* reason why evaluative limitations should be built into self-assessment questionnaires that aim to measure conformity to social stereotypes. A stereotype in itself is neither an attitude nor a moral prescription (Gardner, 1973; Taylor, 1981; Stoppard and Kalin, 1978). While sex stereotypes can certainly have powerful evaluative overtones (cf. Tajfel, 1981), these overtones and the function that they serve are matters for empirical investigation, which can only be hampered by item preselection for social desirability. (Other problems related to social desirability are discussed by Myers and Gonda, 1982a,b; Pedhazui and Tetenbaum, 1979.) Adequate precautions must be taken in operationalizing masculinity and femininity scales to ensure that people have the opportunity of expressing their self-images *vis-à-vis* representative elements of sex stereotypes, whether or not they are the subject of social approval.

The third problem with contemporary MF inventories is that they are operationally insensitive to the possibility of national and regional variation in sex stereotypes, as evidenced by the fact that the criteria against which individual masculinity and femininity are assessed are fixed and invariant, being based loosely on the sex stereotypes of American students. Although there appears to be a great deal of general consensus about the characteristics and behaviours that are seen to be typical of women and men in Western societies (see for example Williams *et al.*, 1977), it is important that this does not attain the status of an assumption before the fact. MF instruments must be ascertained to represent the sex stereotypes of the population on behalf of whom conclusions about the implications of variations in gender identity are drawn.

There is clearly room for improvement upon existing self-categorization measures of masculinity and femininity. The main requirement in order for these improvements to be carried out is a rigorous study of the sex stereotypes, both desirable and undesirable, held by members of the population of interest. Such a study is described below, and the results of this study will be applied to the development of a new procedure for measuring masculinity and femininity in the next chapter.

A Study of Sex Stereotypes and Evaluations

Method

This study was undertaken in Bristol, England, to provide a basis for the development of femininity and masculinity measures that would overcome the shortcomings mentioned above. One hundred and thirty-four students (70 women, 64 men) and 66 non-students (30 women, 36 men), all between the ages of 19 and 26, volunteered to participate in the study, which involved completing five forms of a questionnaire. The forms all consisted of the same 120 personality-descriptive adjectives and differed only in the instructions. On the questionnaires, each adjective was followed by a seven-point rating scale. On the two sex-stereotype forms ('Female Stereotype', FS, and 'Male Stereotype', MS), the seven-point scales were anchored with the labels 'Very Much' and 'Not At All'. On FS and MS, subjects were instructed to 'go through the items, circling the scale point that best indicates the extent to which each is characteristic of WOMEN [or MEN, on MS]'. On the next form, a self-image (SI) questionnaire, they were instructed to mark the items for 'the extent to which each is characteristic of MYSELF'. The last two forms, 'Female Approval' and 'Male Approval' (FA and MA), were measures of social approval, on which the items were anchored with the labels 'Much Approval' and 'Much Disapproval'. On FA subjects were instructed to indicate 'the extent to which WOMEN [MEN on MA] would be met with social approval for acting in the manner described'. Subjects completed MS and FS first and returned them by mail, where upon they were sent SI. When this was returned, they were mailed MA and FA, and finally they were paid £1.00 when these were returned completed. In most cases, all questionnaires were completed within ten days of initial contact.

To ensure that both desirable and undesirable characteristics were represented on the questionnaires, a large pool of items was collected and each one was classified as to whether it had been shown previously to be (1) female- or male-stereotypical, and (2) socially desirable or undesirable. From this initial pool, 80 items were chosen to represent equal proportions of masculine and feminine desirable and undesirable qualities (20 of each kind). The list was supplemented with 40 more items chosen for their stereotypical and /or social desirability characteristics. All items were carefully chosen for clarity of meaning.

Results

The main findings of interest here are those that pertain to the selection of items for the femininity and masculinity scales that will be used in the experiments described in chapter 6 (details can be found in Smith, 1981). The 120 items were first tabulated according to whether they were rated as more stereotypical of women, men, or neither sex on FS and MS. Eighty-four items were rated as reliably sex-stereotypical, using a stringent statistical criterion (see table 5.1).

The results of the analyses of FS and MS were then cross-tabulated with the results of analyses of FA and MA. For each item on FA and MA separately, statistics were calculated to discover if the average social approval rating differed significantly from the midpoint of the seven-point scale. This enabled the items to be classified in terms of whether they were rated as desirable, neutral or undesirable for either or both sexes. The results of this cross-tabulation are given in table 5.1.

It must be emphasized that this cross-tabulation was carried out simply as a means to the end of establishing lists of both socially desirable and undesirable sex-stereotypical items. It should be noted that roughly equal proportions of desirable and undesirable items are subsumed under each sex stereotype. This may well be due to peculiarities of the particular items on the questionnaires, a point that seems to have evaded others who have been quick to conclude that the masculine stereotype is more favoured than the feminine stereotype because more masculine than feminine items on their questionnaire forms were rated as socially desirable (e.g. Rosenkrantz et al., 1968; Pedhazur and Tetenbaum, 1979; see Stoppard, 1976, for an evaluation of this issue).

This study provides a firm empirical foundation for the selection of sex-stereotypical desirable and undesirable questionnaire items valid for a local population, and it will be used to construct the questionnaires described in the next chapter. The procedure adopted here permits the development of a new method of masculinity and femininity measurement that is based upon comparisons between individuals' self-images and their personal sex stereotypes. The method can be compared with other sex stereotype MF measures for its ability to predict some aspects of stereotyping and prejudice.

Despite its potential advantages, however, the present approach is still limited in an important respect: it is based

Table 5.1 A cross-tabulation of items in terms of their sex-stereotypicality and social desirability

1 Masculine Stereotypical Items	2 Feminine Stereotypical Items	3 Non-stereotypical Items
(a) *Desirable for both sexes* Daring, Strong, Competitive, Had leadership abilities, Forward, Logical, Rational, Adventurous, Direct, Decisive, Active, Sense of humour, Independent, Self-confident, Objective, Willing to take a stand, Conventional	(a) *Desirable for both sexes* Neat, Gentle, Well-groomed, Appearance-oriented, Soft-spoken, Sensitive, Tender, Warm, Understanding, Affectionate, Appreciative, Tactful, Likes art and music, Helpful, Mild-mannered, Creative, Conscientious, Co-operative, Dignified, Egalitarian	(a) *Desirable for both sexes* Reliable, Intelligent, Contented, Friendly, Healthy, Competent, Self-sufficient, Interesting, Cheerful, Dependable, Enthusiastic, Adaptable, Sincere, Practical, Likeable, Worldly, Smiling, Persuasive, Attractive, Kind, Self-reliant
(b) *Desirable for men, neutral for women* Willing to take risks, Achievement-oriented, Ambitious	(b) *Desirable for women, neutral for men* Expressive of emotions, Home-oriented	(b) *Undesirable for both sexes* Unsystematic, Solemn, Gives up easily, Useless, Defensive, Wary, Childlike, Inhibited, Seeks revenge, Fussy, Frivolous, Cruel, Jealous
(c) *Desirable for men, undesirable for women* Masculine, Dominant, Hides emotions, Assertive, Tough, Outgoing	(c) *Desirable for women, undesirable for men* Feminine, Emotional, Passive, Shy, Dependent	(c) *Neutral for both sexes* Impulsive
(d) *Neutral for men, undesirable for women* Aggressive, Opinionated	(d) *Neutral for women, undesirable for men* Submissive	(d) *Desirable for women, undesirable for men* Flatterable

Table 5.1 continued

1 Masculine Stereotypical Items	2 Feminine Stereotypical Items	
(e) *Undesirable for both sexes* Coarse Arrogant Uses harsh language Stern Reckless Loud Boastful Feels superior Conceited Severe Egotistical Cynical Autocratic Lazy	(e) *Undesirable for both sexes* Nagging Timid Fearful Unpredictable Gullible Naive Secretive Moody Easily influenced Weak	(f) *Desirable for men, neutral for women* Shrewd (g) *Neutral for both sexes* Theatrical Excitable Subjective

entirely on aspects of disposition or character. We have already mentioned that eventually it will be essential to incorporate other aspects of sex stereotypes into MF measures, including masculine and feminine behaviours, interests, emotions and so on.

6

Judging Masculine and Feminine Social Identities From Speech: Two Experiments

It is apparent, from the great interest that has been displayed in the antecedents, correlates and implications of variations in people's masculine and feminine self-images (see Spence and Helmreich, 1978; Taylor and Hall, 1982; Worell, 1978, for reviews), that men and women do not consider themselves to be uniformly typical/atypical members of their sex group. Rather, they vary enormously in the extent to which their self images correspond to what they believe to be characteristic of men and women in general.

Just as men and women vary in the degree to which they see themselves as conforming to sex-typical norms of personality and behaviour, so they are seen to vary by others. Several of the studies reviewed in chapter 4 suggested that speech-based judgements of masculinity and femininity cannot be reduced to a consideration of the speaker's sex alone, since varying degrees of masculinity and femininity are attributed to both men and women on the basis of a variety of speech cues.

It is virtually unknown, however, whether speech-based attributions of masculinity and femininity bear any resemblance to speaker's self-assessed masculinity and femininity. It is relatively easy to find examples of an hypothesis to the effect that an interactive relationship obtains between people's general expectations and beliefs about men and women, and the behaviour of members of these groups. However, this hypothesis is typically couched in terms of the uniformity of judgemental and evaluative criteria that are brought to bear on individual men and women, and of the uniformity of men's and women's reactions to them. Parsons, Frieze and Ruble (1976) for example, introduced a collection of papers on the topic of the female sex role by emphasizing first the general social components of this interaction, and then the component of individual response:

> Each culture has its own prescriptions of sex-role appropriate behaviours. In the process of acculturation, we come to accept these prescriptions about the roles of men and women as fact; we evaluate ourselves and others in terms of these prescriptions; we raise our children to fit the designated patterns; and we punish deviations from the cultural norm. By providing the evaluative framework for oneself and others, these cultural stereotypes affect men's and women's judgements and beliefs regarding the appropriateness of various roles . . . Women acquire, through a process of socialization, a set of attitudes and beliefs and choices and behaviours which are consistent with the sex roles they are expected to play in society. [pp. 2,3]

In contrast to this rather ironclad caricature of the interaction between social ideology and individual behaviour, Goffman (1977) seems to admit the possibility of a degree of variety, at least at the level of individual response, although the theme of uniformity is still predominant (see quote, p. 22). But what of variations in response to the espousedly monolithic ideology of male–female difference, variations that are manifest at one level in the self-images of men and women? And what of variations in the criteria that are brought to bear on judgements of people's masculinity and femininity that cannot be accounted for in terms of the stimulus person's sex alone? How should the hypothesis of correspondence between general social belief and individual identity be modified to accommodate these variations?

One possibility to be investigated by the experiments described in this chapter is that variations in listeners' speech-based judgements of masculinity and femininity correspond to speakers' own gender identities, as measured by a revised self-categorization MF questionnaire that attempts to overcome the criticisms raised in chapter 5. Another feature of this chapter will be an attempt to discover if reliable patterns of evaluative discrimination accompany the attribution of masculinity and femininity. It is evident from several experiments that deviations from sex-associated beliefs and expectations can have important evaluative consequences.

For example, Harris (1977) asked students to judge several male and female stimulus persons, represented by short written personality descriptions, on several rating scales related to competence and attractiveness. The descriptions of half of the male and half of the female stimulus persons were written so as to be congruent with contemporary sex stereotypes (i.e., males described in stereotypically masculine terms and females in feminine terms, according to a study of sex stereotypes by Williams and Best, 1976), while the other half were counter-stereotypical (i.e. feminine males and masculine females). The social desirability of the adjectives comprising the descriptions was also varied, orthogonally to stimulus person sex and MF. Analysis of the judges' ratings showed that the sex of the stimulus person was less important than either trait favourability or MF in determining judgements of competence and attractiveness:

> Students with favourable traits were rated more highly on all variables, and those with masculine traits were expected to get higher grades, do better in college, and be more intelligent but to be liked less well by teachers and cause more trouble than those with feminine traits [p. 353], [but] . . . the sex of the person being rated did not lead to any significant differences in ratings on the evaluative scales, with the surprising exception that females were rated as more intelligent than males. [pp. 360–1]

In a similar study, Tilby and Kalin (1977) asked psychology students to make judgements about the 'psychological adjustment' of several male and female stimulus persons, again represented by short written descriptions of their occupations, interests and behaviour. The descriptions were composed so that half were congruent with sex stereotypes, and half were counter-stereotypical. Analysis of the judgements showed that

> normal people with sex-role deviant occupations and interests were judged to be less well adjusted than sex role congruent people in the spheres of work and career, family relationships and relationships with friends. They were also judged to be more likely to require psychiatric help sometime within the next ten years. [p. 10]

This effect was particularly strong for male stimulus persons. Unfortunately, these researchers analysed the judgements only in terms of comparisons between sex-role-congruent and -deviant stimulus persons, and do not present results on the independent effects of stimulus person sex and MF. These results, while interesting, are nevertheless based on judgements made about written profiles of fictitious persons. Furthermore, masculinity and femininity were not varied independently in these experiments: stimulus persons were presented as either feminine or masculine, and descriptions of relatively androgynous and undifferentiated gender identities were not used.

An experiment using more realistic stimuli was reported by Lippa, Valdez and Jolly (1983). They videotaped 36 female and 36 male students who had previously completed the BSRI for 30 seconds each as they role-played the part of a high school math teacher describing triangles. Observer subjects then rated these stimulus persons on a seven-point scale anchored by the labels 'Very Feminine' and 'Very Masculine'. One group of observers made their judgements on the basis of the total stimulus information – full video plus voice. Other groups were exposed to only partial information: full video without sound; faces only; body only, or voices only. Observer's ratings were found to be consistently and significantly correlated with the stimulus person's femininity scores, but not with masculinity, a pattern of results that varied little between observational conditions. These results are encouraging, but the use of a single judgemental MF rating scale. and the BSRI, impose severe interpretive constraints, obscuring the reason for the absence of correspondence between speakers' masculinity scores and judgements.

The Experiments

Introduction

In the two experiments that I will describe in the remainder of the chapter, female and male listeners heard the tape-recorded voices of four speakers of each sex reading a short passage of prose, and rated each speaker on several sex-stereotypical personality characteristics. The speakers were chosen especially from among 60 participants in the sex stereotype study described in chapter 5, who had subsequently volunteered to take part in a tape-recorded interview. They were selected on the basis of their responses to the self-image (SI) and sex stereotypes (MS and FS) questionnaires to represent people of both sexes with a wide variety of masculine and feminine self-images. In addition, listeners in Experiment 2 were given the opportunity to make evaluative judgements of the speakers on non-sex-stereotypical personality characteristics related to social competence and attractiveness. Listeners also rated their own masculinity and femininity, using the same set of adjectives on which they rated the speakers. The purpose of this was to enable a preliminary exploration of the possibility that listeners' own masculinity and femininity might influence their perceptions and judgements of others, a topic taken up later in the chapter.

The overriding criticism of the impression-formation-type studies of the preceding chapters that are relevant to the question of perceived masculinity and femininity (e.g. Addington, 1968; Aronovitch, 1976; Edelsky, 1976a,b; McConnell-Ginet, 1978b; Siegler and Siegler, 1976) is that they adopt a particularistic point of departure, manipulating vocal, intonational, paralinguistic or other stylistic variables in isolation, sometimes even in written form. While the need for studies of impressions formed on the basis of particular speech variables may eventually arise, they are premature at a time when it is unknown if reliable impressions of masculinity and femininity are formed on the basis of the undoctored speech of real people. It is, after all, people and not isolated speech variables that are the object of judgemental impressions formed in everyday encounters. This is not to belittle the need for control in studies of social judgement, however; and, given the essentially exploratory nature of these studies, it was deemed necessary to exercise some control over the range of speech variables that could be responsible for variations in listeners' attributions. Accordingly, listeners heard each of the speakers read the same short passage of lively prose, thus eliminating variations arising from factors such as topic, vocabulary, grammar and many of the features described in chapter 4.

It was also considered essential to minimize variation among the speech samples owing to differences in context or setting. Thus, the speech recording surroundings and instructions were kept constant for all speakers. Furthermore, the possible influence of the sex or other characteristics of the interviewer was eliminated by isolating the speakers in a room by themselves for the duration of the recording session. Full printed instructions contained all the information necessary for speakers to complete the task successfully.

Speakers and speech samples

Thirty women and 30 men who had participated in the sex stereotype study subsequently agreed to come to the Department of Psychology and have their voices tape-recorded. From among these 60 tape-recordings, the voices of four women and four men were chosen to represent a speaker of each sex with a relatively masculine gender identity, one each with a relatively feminine gender identity, one each who endorsed relatively high levels of masculinity and femininity as characteristic of him or herself (referred to forthwith as the 'Androgynous Speakers'), and one each who eschewed self-typification in either feminine or masculine terms (called the 'Undifferentiated Speakers').

The eight speakers were chosen on the basis of their self-ratings on the 20 most male-stereotypical characteristics and the 20 most female-stereotypical characteristics from the stereotype study (see table 6.1). Since only 60 of the original 200 participants in the questionnaire study were tape-recorded, speakers could not be found who were maximally representative of the types Masculine, Feminine, Androgynous and Undifferentiated for the sample of 200. The final selection of speakers was made in the attempt to maximize the contrast among speakers of each type on masculinity and femininity within each sex.

Table 6.1 The eight speakers' scores on masculinity and femininity and associated ranks

	M	Rank	F	Rank
Male speakers				
Androgynous	94	2	98	2
Masculine	98	1	44	8
Feminine	62	5	88	4
Undifferentiated	58	6	70	6
Mean and s.d. for sample of 100 men	76±17		76±15	
Female speakers				
Androgynous	72	4	92	3
Feminine	44	7	122	1
Masculine	84	3	58	7
Undifferentiated	34	8	78	5
Mean and s.d. or sample of 100 women	61±20		90±16	

The speakers were tape-recorded as they sat alone reading a short passage of lively prose. These readings were then edited on to a stimulus tape. The order of speakers was: Undifferentiated Male; Undifferentiated Female; Feminine Male, Feminine Female; Masculine Male; Masculine Female; Androgynous Male; and Androgynous Female.

Subjects

The subjects in Experiment 1 were 130 16- and 17-year-old pupils (65 girls, 65 boys) from an English comprehensive school, who participated in two approximately equal-sized consecutive class assembly periods. Subjects in Experiment 2 were 128 students (64 men, 64 women) from several University of Bristol faculties, between the ages of 19 and 25, who volunteered as listener-judges. They participated in groups of between 20 and 25 during lunch hours and after classes.

Materials and procedure

The core element of both experiments was the same. For the judgement task, subjects received a booklet containing eight identical pages for rating the speakers on femininity and masculinity: each page contained five stereotypically masculine items (Coarse; Dominant; Arrogant; Aggressive; Masculine) and five feminine items (Expressive of Emotions; Neat; Nagging; Sensitive; Feminine) in mixed order, each followed by a seven-point rating scale (anchored 'Not at All'–'Very Much'). Subjects in Experiment 2 later received a second booklet containing items related to social competence and attractiveness, which will be described in a subsequent section.

Subjects were told that they would hear the tape-recorded voices of eight people, each reading the same passage of prose, and asked to try to form an impression of what each speaker would be like as a person. When they had a clear impression, they were to rate the speaker on each of the ten scales.

Judgements of masculinity and femininity

Each subject's rating data were reduced to two summary scores for each speaker, by obtaining the sum of the ratings on the five masculinity and five femininity items. Separate three-way $(2 \times 4 \times 2)$ analyses of variance (ANOVAs), with replication on the last factor, were performed on each of these dependent measures for each experiment separately. The independent variables in these analyses were the Sex of the Speaker (Male $v.$ Female), the Type of Speaker (Androgynous, Masculine, Feminine, Undifferentiated) and the Sex of the Listener (Men $v.$ Women), and replicates were subjects.

The ANOVAs on the femininity and masculinity scores in both experiments revealed a consistent absence of significant main and interaction effects involving the Sex of the Listener; male and female subjects did not differ overall in their attributions on these dependent measures. Consistently present in these analyses, however, are significant effects arising from the Sex of the Speaker and the Type of Speaker, and the interaction between these two factors, indicating that attribution of femininity and masculinity to speakers was not governed entirely by either their sex or their gender identity. The results of each of these analyses is described and discussed below with the aid of tables of mean values within each cell of the two-by-four-way interaction between Speaker Sex and Speaker Type. Although Speaker Sex was a potent determinant of attributions, especially of femininity, significant portions of the variance were also due to Speaker Type and to the interaction of these two variables.

In Experiment 1, Male Speakers were rated higher on masculinity overall than were Female Speakers ($\bar{x}$ = 13.03 for males; $\bar{x}$ = 9.52 for females; $F(1, 128)$ = 156.86, p <.001), and Female Speakers were rated higher on femininity ($\bar{x}$ = 18.98 for females and $\bar{x}$ = 13.80 for males; $F(1, 128)$ = 409.90, p <.001). At the level of Speaker Type, Masculine Speakers were judged to be more masculine than Androgynous, Undifferentiated or Feminine Speakers ($\bar{x}$ = 16.59 for Masculine Speakers; $\bar{x}$ = 9.72, 9.43, 9.34 for Androgynous, Undifferentiated and Feminine Speakers, respectively; $F(3, 384)$ = 185.65, p <.001). Androgynous Speakers received the highest ratings on femininity ($\bar{x}$ = 19.02) followed by Undifferentiated and Feminine Speakers ($\bar{x}$ = 16.80 for Undifferentiated Speakers and $\bar{x}$ = 16.35 for Feminine Speakers) and, lastly, Masculine Speakers ($\bar{x}$ = 13,33; $F(3, 384)$ = 126.81, p <.001). These overall patterns of masculinity and femininity judgement in terms of Speaker Sex and Speaker Type are complemented by the emergence of highly significant interactions between the two independent variables ($F (3, 384)$ = 50.42, p <.001 for masculinity; F = 79.42, p <.001 for femininity), which necessitates a speaker-by-speaker breakdown of the judgemental data, presented in table 6.2.

The Masculine Male was judged to be the most masculine speaker, followed by the Masculine Female, the Undifferentiated Male and the Androgynous Male. Rated progressively less masculine were the Feminine Female, the Feminine Male and the Androgynous and Undifferentiated Females.

The Undifferentiated Female, besides being rated as the least masculine, was also seen as the most feminine speaker. Also, the Masculine Male, seen as the most masculine, was rated as the least feminine. However, the attribution of femininity is not simply the inverse of the attribution of masculinity as far as these

Table 6.2   Means within cells of the interaction between Sex of
Speaker and Type of Speaker for judgements of masculinity and
femininity in Experiment 1*

Sex of Speaker	*Type of Speaker* Androgynous	Masculine	Feminine	Undifferentiated
Masculinity				
Male	10.89b	20.44a	9.02bc	11.76b
Female	8.55bc	12.75b	9.66bc	7.11c
Femininity				
Male	19.13a	9.02c	13.52b	13.38b
Female	18.91a	17.63a	19.18a	20.21a

*Means that share any element of a subscript in common do not differ significantly at
$p = 0.05$; all tests made using Tukey's HSD test, standard error of measurement
associated with one treatment mean $(Sw^2) = 0.51$; $df = 3$ for masculinity, and 0.42,
$df = 3$ for femininity.

listener-judges are concerned, and mirror-image congruency
between masculinity and femininity attributions occur only at
each extremity. Thus, the second most feminine speaker was seen
to be not the Androgynous Female, but rather the Feminine
Female, followed closely by the Androgynous Male and the
Androgynous Female. The Masculine Female, and the Feminine,
Undifferentiated and Masculine Males, were rated progressively
less feminine.

The patterns of femininity and masculinity attribution that
emerged in Experiment 2 are very similar to those described
above. Indeed, the rank-order correlation between the mean
attributions of femininity to Speakers in Experiments 1 and 2 is
significant ($p\bar{x} = .98$, $N = 8$, $p <.001$, as is that between mean
attributions of masculinity ($p\bar{x} = .95$, $N = 8$, $p <.01$).

In Experiment 2, Male Speakers were judged to be more
masculine than Female Speakers ($\bar{x} = 18.83$ for males; $\bar{x} = 14.83$
for females; $F(1,126) = 210.28$, $p <.001$), and the Masculine
Speakers were rated higher on masculinity than Androgynous,
Feminine or Undifferentiated Speakers ($\bar{x}$ 23.47 for Masculine
Speakers and $\bar{x} = 15.43$, 14.26, 14.16 for Androgynous,
Feminine and Undifferentiated Speakers, respectively;

F (3,378)= 285.90, p <.001). From the table of means for the significant two-way interaction of Speaker Sex with Speaker Type (F (3,378) = 21.80, p <.001; see table 6.3), it can be seen that the Masculine Male and Masculine Female were judged most masculine, followed by the Androgynous, Undifferentiated and Feminine Males. The Feminine, Androgynous and Undifferentiated Female Speakers were rated as least masculine.

Table 6.3   Means within cells of the interaction between Speaker Sex and Speaker Type for judgements of masculinity and femininity in Experiment 2*

| Sex of Speaker | Type of speaker | | | |
	Androgynous	Masculine	Feminine	Undifferentiated
Masculinity				
Male	18.63bc	25.41a	14.73cde	16.55cd
Female	12.23de	21.54ab	13.79de	11.77e
Femininity				
Male	22.58a	13.66c	16.75bc	16.29bc
Female	23.51a	19.52b	23.95a	24.01a

*Means that share any element of a subscript in common do not differ at p = 0.05; all tests made using Tukey's HSD test, (Sw^2) = 0.51, df = 3 or masculinity and 0.42, df = 3 for femininity.

Female Speakers were judged to be more feminine than Male Speakers ($\bar{x}$ = 22.75 for females and $\bar{x}$ = 17.32 for males; F(1,126) = 481.45, p <.001), and the Androgynous Speakers were rated as most feminine ($\bar{x}$ = 23.04) followed by the Feminine and Undifferentiated Speakers ($\bar{x}$ = 20.35 and 20.15, respectively), with Masculine Speakers receiving the lowest femininity ratings ($\bar{x}$ = 16.59; F(3,378) = 157.75, p <.001). These generalities are complicated by the two-way interaction between Speaker Sex and Speaker Type (F(3,378) = 53.48, p <.001 – means are presented in table 6.3, which shows that the Undifferentiated, Feminine and Androgynous Females, and the Male, received the highest femininity ratings, followed by the Masculine Female, the Feminine and Undifferentiated Males.

The correspondence between speakers' perceived
and self-assessed femininity and masculinity

In order to examine the correspondence between speakers' self-assessed masculinity and femininity and listeners' speech-based impressions of speakers' masculinity and femininity, speakers were assigned ranks according to (1) their perceived masculinity and femininity from tables 6.2 and 6.3; and (2) their self-rated masculinity and femininity from table 6.1. Spearman rank correlation coefficients ($\rho\bar{x}$) were calculated between perceived and self-assessed masculinity and femininity for each experiment separately. Statistically significant correlations were obtained in both experiments ($\rho\bar{x} = .67$, $N = 8$, $p < .05$ for masculinity and $\rho\bar{x} = .67$, $p < .05$ for femininity in Experiment 1; $\rho\bar{x} = .81$, $p < .05$ for masculinity, and $\rho\bar{x} = .65$, $p < .05$ for femininity in Experiment 2), indicating reliable overall agreement between perceived and self-rated masculinity and femininity.

These results show that, as expected, people form very reliable impressions of others' femininity and masculinity on the basis of speech alone. Even more important is the demonstration of a significant overall relation between the social perception and self-image of gender identity.

Though optimism must be guarded pending clarification and extension of these findings, the positive results obtained are a step towards illuminating the relationship between one aspect of social identity and social attribution. A person's sex is manifestly not the only or even the most important determinant of inferences about conformity to sex-stereotypical norms of behaviour and demeanour. Furthermore, even short, content-controlled samples of speech are sufficiently informative to enable the formation of impressions that bear a marked, albeit modest, resemblance to people's self-characterizations. While it is of course a matter for empirical attention, it would be difficult to believe that speech uttered under less constrained more familiar circumstances would diminish rather than enhance the strength of this association.

Enthusiasm over these findings is tempered somewhat by the fact that the correlation between speakers' masculinity and femininity and that attributed to them is not perfect. This reminds us that much of the variability in masculinity and femininity attribution cannot be accounted for in terms of speakers' gender identities alone. However, despite the fact that the vagaries of listeners' reactions are determined largely by speaker idiosyncracies not controlled for here, reliable regularities emerge that can be traced to speakers' self-images.

Judgements of competence and attractiveness

After they had completed the ratings for femininity and masculinity, subjects in Experiment 2 were given a second booklet, again containing eight indentical pages, for rating each speaker on items related to social competence and social attractiveness. Four non-sex-stereotypical items were chosen to comprise an index of perceived social competence (the C Scale: Intelligent; Competent; Fluent; Clear), and four more were chosen to comprise an index of social attractiveness (the A Scale: Friendly; Interesting; Reliable; Sincere). Without warning, subjects were asked to listen to the stimulus tape a second time, and to rate the speakers on these eight new items. The rating data on these items were reduced to two summary scores for each speaker, by obtaining the sum of the ratings on the four C and four A items.

Analyses of these data were carried out by means of three-way ANOVAs identical to those used in the analyses of femininity and masculinity above. The analyses of the C and A scores also revealed significant judgemental variations owing to Speaker Sex, Speaker Type and the interaction of these two factors. Surprisingly, Female Speakers are judged to be more competent than Male Speakers ($\bar{x} = 19.13$ for females; $\bar{x} = 16.10$ for males; $F(1,126) = 175.99$, $p < .001$). With respect to Speaker Type, Androgynous Speakers are rated highest on C ($\bar{x} = 21.09$), followed by the Undifferentiated, Masculine and Feminine Speakers ($\bar{x} = 17.09$, 16.89 and 15.38, respectively). The results of the two-way interaction ($F(3,378) = 213.12$, $p < .001$: see table 6.4) reveal that the most competent speakers are judged to be the Androgynous Male and the Feminine and Androgynous Females, followed by the Masculine and Undifferentiated

Females and Males. The Feminine Male is seen as least competent.

Female Speakers are rated higher on A than are Males ($\bar{x}$ = 18.19 for females; $\bar{x}$ = 15.73 for males; $F(1,126)$ = 90.10, p <.001), and Androgynous and Undifferentiated Speakers are rated higher than Feminine and Masculine Speakers ($\bar{x}$ = 18.14 and 17.91 for Androgynous and Undifferentiated Speakers; $\bar{x}$ = 16.48 and 17.30 for Feminine and Masculine Speakers; $F(3,378)$ = 32.85, p <.001). Within the cells of the two-way interaction ($F(3,378$ = 6.57, p <.05: see table 6.5), the most attractive speakers are seen to be the Undifferentiated, Androgynous, and Feminine Females, followed by the Androgynous and Undifferentiated Males and the Masculine Female. Judged lowest on attractiveness are the Feminine and Masculine Males. These results must also be interpreted with considerable caution, based as they are on only eight speakers and in a university context. Nevertheless, it is interesting that females were judged, on average, to be both more competent and more attractive on the basis of speech alone.

Table 6.4 Means within cells of the interaction between Speaker Sex and Speaker Type for judgements of competence and attractiveness in Experiment 2*

| | | Type of Speaker | | |
Sex of Speaker	Androgynous	Masculine	Feminine	Undifferentiated
Competence				
Male	22.61a	15.75b	9.34c	16.68b
Female	19.56ab	18.02b	21.42a	17.51b
Attractiveness				
Male	17.48abc	14.27c	14.59bc	16.55abc
Female	18.78a	16.32abc	18.38ab	19.27a

*Means that share any element of a subscript in common do not differ at p = 0.05; all tests made using Tukey's HSD test (Sw2) = 0.45, df = 3, for competence, and 0.44, df = 3 for attractiveness.

In order to examine in greater depth the relation among judgements of masculinity, femininity, competence and attractiveness in Experiment 2, correlation coefficients were calculated among these four dependent measures for Female and Male Speakers separately (see table 6.5). Overall, judgements of

Table 6.5   Correlation among judgements of masculinity (M), femininity (F), competence (C) and attractiveness (A)

	M	F	C	A
M		−41**	−05	−27**
F	−31**		26**	35**
C	15**	21**		46**
A	−06	24**	48**	

* p < .05   ** p < .01
N = 520, df = 518. Coefficients above the diagonal are for female speakers, and those below for male speakers.

masculinity and femininity are negatively correlated with each other for speakers of both sexes. Since this pattern emerged in a context that included speakers with a variety of gender identities, it strongly suggests that, as far as social perception goes, masculinity and femininity are seen to stand in inverse relation to each other. In the next section we will examine the interaction of self-assessed masculinity and femininity among listeners.

The correlations obtained among judgements of masculinity and femininity and competence and attractiveness are very interesting. For female speakers, perceived femininity is correlated positively with judgements of both competence and attractiveness and masculinity correlates negatively with attractiveness. Thus, in this experiment women were not penalized for femininity – it enhanced both perceived competence and attractiveness. Even for males, perceived femininity enhanced judgements of competence and attractiveness!

Listeners' masculinity and femininity and their judgements of others

At the very outset of Experiment 2, subjects were asked to complete a short self-image questionnaire that was designed as a rudimentary measure of gender identity. This questionnaire consisted of 10 from among the 15 most male-stereotypical items for the sex stereotype study (chapter 5), and 10 of the 15 most female-stereotypical, plus 8 additional non-stereotypical items (those on the C and A Scales) that were included to mask the sex-stereotypical content of the questionnaire. This measure was obtained with a view to examining the possibility of a relation between listeners' femininity and masculinity and their judgements of others.

Thinking along these lines was stimulated by recent experimental research in the social psychology of relations between groups (Tajfel, 1978a, 1981, 1982; Turner and Giles, 1981). Much of this research has investigated the relation between individuals' identification with social groups, and the way in which they perceive and evaluate members of their own and other groups. Many experiments have shown that, under certain conditions, merely assigning people to arbitrary groups can lead to intergroup stereotyping, prejudice and discrimination (Tajfel, 1981; Turner, 1982). Similar observations have been made in many field situations, embracing the familiar topics of racism, ethnocentrism and sexism, among others.

The psychological processes underlying the dynamics of intergroup relations are still not well understood, but some tentative conclusions have been drawn. Turner (1982), for example, argues that: 'under conditions where individuals' social category memberships are salient, they tend to be assigned all the characteristics perceived to define their category'. He hypothesizes that the salience of group membership will affect self-perception just as it does the perception of ingroup and outgroup members. As a particular social categorization becomes more salient, people will tend to perceive themselves as more like the ingroup and less like the outgroup – in other words, they self-stereotype.

On the face of it, these hypotheses seem to suggest that, in the context of female–male relations, feminine and masculine gender identity will be related systematically to judgements in the impression-formation task. Specifically, it could be hypothesized that the stronger is ingroup gender identity (higher femininity and/or lower masculinity for females; vice versa for males), the greater will be the tendency to stereotype speakers on the basis of their sex in the impression-formation task. This relation could be manifest in terms of a tendency to attribute masculine characteristics unilaterally to male speakers and feminine characteristics to females, or simply by a tendency to exaggerate similarities among speakers of the same sex (i.e. to ignore within-sex individual differences) and to exaggerate differences between sexes.

On the other hand, the primary emphasis in the above-mentioned research tradition has so far been on the effects of experimental manipulations and situational variables on social perception and judgement (Turner, 1982). Thus it can be shown that an experimental manipulation of group salience influences the *average* level of self and other stereotyping of people in the experimental group (e.g. Doise, 1978), but the question remains as to whether this relation can also be observed at the individual level. It could be suggested that the salience of sex group membership and gender identity are not the same thing. Experiments have shown that a crucial variable in determining salience is the *security* of social identity that is, the degree to which one's identity is perceived to be contributing positively and reliably to one's self-esteem (e.g. Bagely, 1978; Turner and Brown, 1978). The evidence to date indicates that security and salience are inversely related: the more secure is identity, the less salient is group membership, and hence the less intergroup stereotyping, prejudice and discrimination. Transposing this to the male–female context, the question is, what is the relation between gender identity and security? If they are positively correlated, then the strength of ingroup gender identity will presumably correlate negatively with the tendency to stereotype speakers on the basis of sex, contrary to our first hypotheses. Of course, it is also possible that security and gender identity are not systematically related, in which case no systematic effects of masculinity and femininity on impression formation would be predicted.

Sixty-two men and 48 women completed the SI questionnaire at the outset of Experiment 2. Two kinds of masculinity and femininity scores were calculated for each of these subjects. The first, called 'fixed-criterion' masculinity and femininity, were calculated by taking the sum of a subject's self-ratings on the masculinity and femininity items, respectively, from SI. These scores are similar to those obtained on the BSRI, but are more refined, being based on locally valid sex stereotypes.

The second kind of masculinity and femininity score was based on a variable criterion. For each subject, the absolute difference was calculated between their self-image on SI and their ratings of each of the male speakers, and each of the female speakers. This resulted in eight difference scores, each based on 10 items. This procedure is illustrated in table 6.6.

Table 6.6 An example of the calculation of a difference score

Item	Judgements of Speaker A	Self-image	Difference
Neat	5	5	0
Coarse	3	2	1
Expressive	2	4	2
Dominant	2	2	0
Nagging	3	2	1
Aggressive	2	1	1
Sensitive	2	5	3
Arrogant	3	2	1
Feminine	3	3	0
Masculine	5	5	0
			—
Difference Score			9

The sum of the four difference scores between SI and ratings of the Male Speakers was called Personal M, and the sum of the four difference scores between SI and ratings of the Female Speakers was called Personal F. These scores represent the difference between a person's self-image and their perceptions of the male and female stimulus persons, and are more direct measures of social identification with members of one's own and the other sex group than are the fixed-criterion measures.

It should be noted that, since these are difference scores, increases in them represent *decreases* in whichever aspect of gender identity is being measured, unlike the fixed-criterion scores, on which increases represent increasing strength of masculinity or femininity. The signs (+ or −) of all correlations involving either Personal M or Personal F and other variables have been reversed in the results given in tables 6.8 and 6.9 thus making them directly comparable to correlations involving fixed-criteron masculinity and femininity.

A direct measure of the security of gender identity was not obtained in this experiment. However, a rough measure of self-esteem was available from subjects' self-ratings on the eight socially desirable, non-stereotypical items on the self-image questionnaire representing social competence and attractiveness: the higher a subject's self-image on these items, the more positively they think of themselves.

In order to examine the relations among listeners' gender identities and the attribution of masculinity and femininity to others along the lines described here, two new sets of difference scores were calculated for each listener. The first set represents the perceived differences between all possible pairs of speakers on the ten MF items. For any pair, the difference score is just the absolute difference between ratings given to Speaker A and Speaker B, summed across the ten items. This procedure yielded 28 scores per subject, which were then reduced to 3 subscores: the sum of the 6 between-male scores; the sum of the 6 between-female scores; and the sum of the difference scores between the 16 male–female speaker comparisons. Each of these scores was then divided by the total sum of the difference scores and multiplied by 100, resulting in three percentage scores representing the percentage of differentiation among speakers for each subject owing to (1) perceived differences among male speakers ($\male$); (2) perceived differences among female speakers ($\female$); and (3) perceived male–female differences ($\male$–$\female$).

These scores reflect individual differences in the tendency to differentiate among speakers of the same sex and between speakers of opposite sex on stereotypical items. They do not, however, directly reflect the degree to which masculinity characteristics are attributed unilaterally to male speakers and femininity characteristics to females. Therefore a fourth score, called the $\male$M–$\female$F score, designed to reflect this, was calculated for each subject.

The second set of difference scores was calculated to represent evaluative differences between the speakers on the competence and attractiveness items. Twenty-eight scores were calculated for each subject in the same way as those described above (except that each was based on the 8 competence and attractiveness items instead of the 10 masculinity and femininity items), and these were then reduced to three subscores representing the percentage of the total evaluative differentiation among speakers owing to: (1) differentiation among male speakers ($\male E$); (2) differentiation among female speakers ($\female E$); and (3) differentiation between male and female speakers ($\male-\female E$).

These scores reflect individual differences in the tendency to differentiate among speakers on evaluative items, but they do not necessarily reflect the tendency to make more positive judgements about speakers of one sex or the other. Thus, an eighth score was calculated, as the difference between the sum of ratings of male speakers on the competence and attractiveness items, and the sum of ratings of female speakers on these items. This score will be symbolized, $\male+-\female+$.

The means and standard deviations of fixed-criterion and Personal M and F, Self-esteem, and the eight differentiation

Table 6.7 Means and standard deviations of men and women on the M and F variables and the eight differentiation scores

| | Men (N = 62) | | Women (N = 48) | |
	x	s.d.	x	s.d.
Fixed M	19.3	4.2	12.3	4.4
Fixed F	16.1	4.0	21.0	3.8
Personal M	71.6	16.9	73.7	21.6
Personal F	73.9	19.4	71.9	20.4
Self-esteem	39.8	6.3	40.6	7.9
♂	20.0	3.5	19.1	3.4
♀	18.6	4.0	18.3	3.6
♂-♀	61.4	5.6	62.5	4.7
♂M-♀F	29.6	21.7	32.8	22.0
♂E	23.0	4.6	22.4	4.6
♀E	20.0	4.9	19.8	5.2
♂-♀E	57.0	5.2	57.8	3.8
♂+-♀+	−22.4	19.5	−27.0	19.9

Table 6.8 Correlations among measures of masculinity and femininity and indices of differentiation

	Fixed M	Fixed F	Personal M	Personal F	Self-esteem	♂	♀	♂–♀	♂M–♀F	♂E	♀E	♂–♀E	♂+–♀+
Fixed M		23	-18	26	31*	-03	24	-18	-19	-22	29*	-06	-03
Fixed F	-09		-21	28*	67**	-28	34*	-03	03	-25	21	11	-12
Personal M	01	31*		-10	-14	16	-49**	23	30*	64**	-44**	-37**	50**
Personal F	-21	20	-20		32*	-16	47**	-23	-28*	-61**	57**	15	34*
Self-esteem	-19	26*	20	-35**		-21	31	-06	-16	-26	27	04	-14
♂	21	00	27*	20	03		-14	-67**	-58**	10	11	27	39**
♀	11	-05	14	08	03	12		-64**	-48**	-42**	32*	22	-39**
♂–♀	-21	04	-27*	12	-04	-71**	-78**		81**	23	-33*	06	02
♂M–♀F	-19	09	-20	-55**	-16	-51**	-69**	87**		30*	-30*	-06	06
♂E	-00	04	51**	54**	-03	48**	-20	-17	14			-53**	52**
♀E	-19	01	-48**	06	10	-49**	15	20	21	-73**		-22	05
♂–♀E	-01	-09	03	-13	04	-04	14	-07	-03	-01	-02		-79**
♂+–♀+	-24	10	01		-14	08	-26**	13	12	29*	13	-53**	

* p < .05   ** p < .01

Correlations above the diagonal are for female listeners (N = 48, df = 46) and those below are for male listeners (N = 62, df = 60). For ease of interpretation, the signs of all correlations between Personal M and F and other variables have been reversed.

scores are given in table 6.7, and the correlations among them in table 6.8

It can be seen from table 6.8 that the fixed-criterion and Personal M and F measures are not strongly related. It can also be seen that Personal M and F are much more often closely related to the measures of within- and between-group differentiation than are the fixed-criterion measures. In order to assess the relations among gender identity, self-esteem and the differentiation measures, mulitple linear regression analyses were calculated between the predictor variables, M, F and Self-esteem, and the criterion variables, ♂, ♀, ♂–♀, ♂M–♀F, ♂E, ♀E, ♂–♀E, ♂+–♀+. A multiple regression analysis calculates the strength of association between the predictor variables and the criterion variable, adjusting the product–moment correlations in table 6.8 to take account of the correlations among the predictor variables. Under certain conditions, the predictive strength of a group of predictor variables taken together will exceed that of any of the variables taken alone. A multiple regression analysis, then, will help to clarify what, if any, predictive advantages are to be gained from considering the interrelations among M, F and Self-esteem.

None of the analyses performed using the fixed-criterion M and F scores resulted in statistically significant multiple regression coefficients. Furthermore, the criterion variables are not significantly correlated with any of these predictor variables among male subjects, and only sporadically among female subjects.

The analyses performed using Personal M and F scores, on the other hand, produced several significant multiple regression coefficients to supplement a pattern of associations that is in some ways consistent with, and in other ways different from, those predicted by the hypothesis that the strength of gender identity is correlated with the security of gender identity. These results are given in table 6.9. Taking the consistencies first, the associations between M and F, and ♂–♀, ♂M–♀F, ♂–♀E and ♂+–♀+ are in the directions predicted, although several of the correlations do not reach statistical significance. In general, the strength of ingroup gender identity (increasing masculinity and decreasing femininity for male subjects; vice versa for females) is associated

Table 6.9   Results of multiple linear regression analyses between masculinity, femininity, self-esteem and indices of differentiation

Criterion variables	Personal M Partial		Personal F Partial		Self-esteem Partial		R^2	F
	r	t	r	t	r	t		
Male subjects								
♂	.23	1.81	−.32	−2.59**	.11	0.87	.17	4.09**
♀	.19	1.47	.23	1.84	.04	0.33	.08	1.59
♂–♀	−.27	−2.16*	.04	0.29	−.09	−0.72	.08	1.74
♂M–♀F	−.20	−1.55	.10	0.71	−.14	1.07	.06	1.31
♂E	.51	4.49**	−.54	−4.85**	.13	1.01	.48	17.95**
♀E	−.45	−3.82**	.52	4.63**	−.03	−0.22	.44	15.04**
♂–♀E	.03	0.26	.07	0.53	−.04	−0.31	.01	0.14
♂+–♀+	−.02	−0.12	−.14	−1.09	.11	0.81	.03	0.58
Female subjects								
♂	.09	0.61	−.02	−0.13	.19	1.27	.07	1.03
♀	−.30	−2.07*	.17	1.14	−.23	−1.56	.32	6.88**
♂–♀	.10	0.70	−.11	0.76	−.01	−0.04	.07	1.03
♂M–♀F	.17	1.12	−.10	−0.64	.09	0.61	.11	1.85
♂E	.43	3.17**	−.29	−2.03*	.14	0.97	.50	14.44**
♀E	−.13	−0.87	.37	2.67**	−.13	−0.87	.34	7.65**
♂–♀E	−.36	−2.55**	−.12	−0.78	−.02	−0.15	.15	2.57
♂+–♀+	.40	2.88**	−.01	0.00	.07	0.49	.26	5.07**

$* p < .05$ $** p < .01$
Partial r = partial correlation; t = t-statistic for significance of partial r ($N = 62$, $df = 61$ for men; $N = 48$, $df = 47$ for women); R = coefficient of multiple determination for combined correlation of three predictor variables with the criterion variable; F = F-ratio for significance of R ($df = 3, 61$ for men; $df = 3, 47$ for women). For ease of interpretation, the signs of all partial rs have been reversed.

with a *decreasing* tendency to differentiate between the sexes on the variables ♂–♀, ♂M–♀F and ♂–♀E. For ♂+–♀+ among females, increasing masculinity is significantly correlated with the tendency to polarize evaluations of the speakers on the competence and attractiveness items in favour of male speakers.

On the variables ♂, ♀, ♂E and ♀E, the pattern of associations is consistently at variance with those described above in an interesting and important way. Instead of gender identity being associated with the tendency to view both ingroup and outgroup members less stereotypically, the strength of gender identity correlates with a tendency to differentiate among speakers of one's own sex group, while at the same time rating speakers of the other group more homogeneously, both in the attribution of characteristics related to MF, and on the C and A scales.

Put simply, the results of these analyses suggest that listeners discriminate less between male and female speakers, perceive members of their own sex as less uniform, and members of the opposite sex as more uniform, as the strength of ingroup gender identity increases.

It should be noted, however, that there is only weak evidence in this experiment linking the *strength* of gender identity with the *security* of gender identity. It can be seen from table 6.8 that the self-esteem measure is correlated only weakly with the strength of gender identity (increasing Personal M and decreasing F for men, vice-versa for women). It is also clear from the results of the regression analyses that the self-esteem variable does not play an important role in these associations. It must be recalled, though, that a comprehensive and reliable measure of self-esteem was not taken in this experiment. Thus, the relations observed among M, F and Self-esteem, weak as they may be, are encouraging. Certainly, they will stimulate more research along these lines.

7

The Management of Interaction

Up to this point we have considered the role of language as a vehicle for the representation of women and men (chapter 3), as a marker of sex class, and subsequently as a basis for the attribution of masculinity and femininity (chapter 4) and the expression of gender identity (chapters 5 and 6). In this chapter we turn to consider the use of language to regulate interpersonal interaction between men and women, that is, as a resource base that can be strategically managed in the pursuit of communication goals. The aim is to develop understanding about the impact of the sexual subculture on the interpersonal conduct of women and men; and, as usual, the realization of this aim is severely hampered by the exclusive preoccupation with sex differences.

Nevertheless, there is considerable evidence that the norms of femininity and masculinity encourage women and men to construe communication situations and the goals of interaction somewhat differently. These differences are best described with reference to studies that have sought to discover the psychological dimensions that underlie people's conceptions of: (1) individual differences in interpersonal style; (2) social stituations; and (3) social episodes.

Two main dimensions that emerge from these studies, and that account for most of the variation in the data, have been termed 'control' and 'affiliation'. The control dimension, which orders people, situations and episodes in terms of the extent to which they provide the opportunity for exerting active control over the process and outcomes of interaction, is highly correlated with traditional conceptions of masculinity. The affiliation dimension orders people, situations and episodes in terms of their tendency to elicit warmth and approach versus aloofness and avoidance. This dimension is highly correlated with the traditional norms of femininity. Thus, it could be hypothesized that individual differences in masculinity and femininity will be related to variations in the management of control– and affiliation-related resources respectively. Moreover, if we are prepared to accept the premise that femininity is in general the more important component of women's gender identity, and masculinity of men's, we might also expect women to be more concerned with the communicative goal of affiliation, and men to be preoccupied with aspects of control. Finally, the normative demands of the particular situation in which interaction occurs may often confer asymmetrical advantages upon those with different communication skills, leading to the prediction that reactions to situations that demand the modulation of control-related resources will be better predicted by masculinity (and hence more adeptly managed by men overall), while reactions to affiliative situations will be better predicted by femininity (and more skilfully handled by women).

These hypotheses are supported by a great variety of evidence pertaining to the management of specific communication resources, which range from so-called powerless speech to conversational dominance, tactics of persuasion, content, self-disclosure and conflict management.

This formulation causes us to revise our thinking about sex differences in communication. Researchers have tended to think of these differences in terms of bipolar contrasts, usually defined as dominant–muted or powerful–powerless, with men occupying the 'dominant' end and women the 'muted' end of the continuum. In contrast, the present formulation leads us to think in terms of two independent, intersecting dimensions that consist of norms prescribing the preoccupations of masculinity (control) and femininity (affiliation), respectively. Men are not 'dominant' and women 'muted': rather, men, who are encouraged to be masculine, are concerned to manage and monitor the control-related aspects of interaction; while women, encouraged to be feminine, will tend to manage and monitor interaction in the pursuit of affiliative goals. Now I will develop these arguments in more detail.

Dimensions of Interpersonal Conduct: Affiliation and Control

Personality: the interpersonal domain

We have already seen (chapter 3) that the gender formulae for masculinity and femininity order expectations about the sexes in ways that have important implications for communication. At the group level of contrast, the implications of being female or male seem often to place the sexes at opposite poles of a single dimension: deviant–normal; domestic political; low status–high status and so on (chapter 3, pp. 55–6). Contrasts that pertain to interpersonal behaviour are less obviously bipolar, however. Femininity is associated with communality, expressivity, nurturance and affiliation. Masculinity is connected with agency, intrumentality, dominance and control.

According to some personality theorists, these constructs have a significance far beyond the domain of the sexual subculture; indeed, they are considered to be the two major dimensions underlying our perception of the entire domain of interpersonal behaviour. Wiggins (1979), for example, building on the work of interpersonal theorists of personality (e.g. Leary, 1957; Sullivan, 1953), compiled a taxonomy of trait-descriptive terms that pertain to interpersonal behaviour by classifying them into categories of similar behaviours. This classification proceeded according to an explicit model, which conceptualizes the domain of interpersonal behaviour to be organized around two orthogonal, intersecting dimensions. One dimension is defined by the bipolar contrasts, ambitious/dominant–lazy/submissive, while the other is anchored by the contrasts, warm/agreeable–cold/quarrelsome. Other contrasts are ordered around the two-dimensional space defined by the two major dimensions, in the circular manner depicted in figure 7.1, resulting in a so-called 'interpersonal circle'. Each pole of these contrasts corresponds to a scale comprised of several trait-descriptive terms. For example, some traits on Wiggins's Dominance scale are 'dominant', 'forceful', 'assertive' and 'firm', while traits on the Warm scale are 'tender', 'kind', 'emotional' and 'sympathetic'. Wiggins presents an impressive array of evidence from factor-analytical studies to show that the two-dimensional circular structure (called a circumplex), is very closely approximated by subjects' self-descriptions using the 128 (16 scales × 8 items per scale) adjectives on his Interpersonal Adjective Scales (IAS).

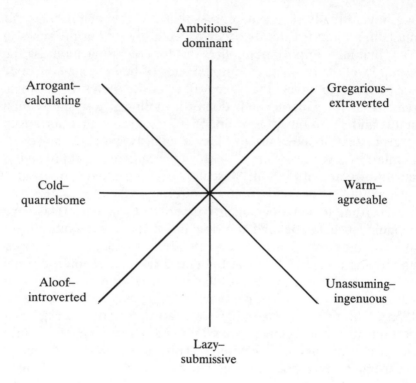

Figure 7.1 The circumplex model of interpersonal behaviour (after Wiggins, 1982)

The IAS is, from a psychometric point of view, the best of several personality measures that capitalize on the circumplex approach to the description of interpersonal behaviour. The theoretical requirements of such a measure are enumerated by Kiesler (1983), who writes:

The circular array represents a two-dimensional Euclidean space reflecting the joint action of two basic interpersonal dimensions or motivations, almost universally designated

Control and Affiliation. These dimensions define, respectively, the vertical and horizontal axes of the circle. A large body of research reviewed by Berzins (1977), Bierman (1969), Carson (1969), DeVogue and Beck (1978), Foa (1961) and Wiggins (1982) convincingly demonstrates that interpersonal behaviour represents the joint expression of these two underlying dimensions. Hence, this criterion reflects the assumption that pairs of interactants, in their daily transactions, are negotiating mutually satisfactory definitions regarding who is going to be more or less in control or dominant and what is to be the characteristic level of friendliness or hostility. [p. 186]

Wiggins is careful to point out that 'structural relationships of the kind at issue here are not "discovered". They are postulated and then evaluated for goodness of fit' (p. 400). That the model fits the facts of self-descriptions of interpersonal behaviour, and also theory and data from a wide variety of related studies (Kiesler, 1983; Wiggins, 1980; 1982), so well strongly suggests, however, that the dimensions of control and affiliation are fundamental to our thinking about interpersonal behaviour in general.

The relevance of this model to conceptions of masculinity and femininity was explicity examined by Wiggins and Holzmuller (1978). They noted that virtually all of the items on the BSRI Masculinity scale are related to the dominant–ambitious vector of the IAS circumplex, while most of the feminine items fall within the warm–agreeable vector. In order to examine the relations between Bem's measures of masculinity and femininity, and the IAS scales, they analysed data from 187 students who had completed a lengthy personality questionnaire that included the IAS items. (Correlations between the BSRI-similar scales used in this analysis and the actual BSRI masculinity and femininity scales were .97 and .92, based on the responses of an additional sample of 110 students.) The highest correlations between the femininity scale and IAS variables were with the cold–quarrelsome (−.609) and warm–agreeable (.750) scales, while the highest correlations for masculinity were with the dominant–ambitious (.797) and lazy–submissive (−.600) scales. These results received additional support in a later study (Wiggins and

Holzmuller, 1981), in which the viability of alternative measures of masculinity and femininity, based on the four pairs of orthogonal contrasts in figure 7.1 (gregarious–extraverted *v*. arrogant–calculating; lazy–submissive *v*. cold–quarrelsome; unassuming–ingenuous *v*. aloof–introverted; ambitious–dominant *v*. warm–agreeable) was tested by examining their ability to discriminate the responses of women and men, and also to differentiate sex-typed from androgynous individuals of each sex. As we would predict, the most satisfactory contrast in this respect was ambitious–dominant *v*. warm–agreeable.

This evidence leads one to conclude that the concepts of masculinity and femininity embodied in the BSRI are based on highly generalizable personal constructs, which are furthermore the best available combination of orthogonal contrasts from the IAS. These encouraging conclusions do not diminish the concerns about the BSRI as a measurement tool voiced in chapter 5, but they do provide a considerable degree of convergence on the centrality of the control and affiliation constructs to conceptions of masculinity and femininity.

Another basis for this inference can be gleaned from examining again the sex stereotypes obtained from the study described in chapter 5 (table 5.1). Although it was unfortunately not a priority of this study, or of the experiment reported in chapter 6 to investigate the interpersonal domain, it is clear that the vectors of the IAS circumplex most pertinent to the masculine stereotype are ambitious–dominant and arrogant–calculating, while those most pertinent to the feminine stereotypes are warm–agreeable and unassuming–ingenuous.

The significance of these observations is that they lead us beyond the important but restricted focus on the role-related consequences of sex class membership, to consider the impact of variations in gender identity on communication. They also cause us to question models of sex differences in interaction that rely simply upon placing feminine and masculine tactics at opposite ends of a singular bipolar continuum, such as dominant–muted, powerful–powerless or assertive–submissive. The picture that emerges here sharpens Constantinople's (1973) objection to the bipolar conception of MF (see chapter 5). It appears that, in our society, the norms of femininity and masculinity pertain to separate, uncorrelated dimensions of conduct, at least in the interpersonal domain. Whether the same will be found to hold true in other domains (e.g. temperament, character, mood, intellectual qualities, attitudes, interests, etc) remains an important research question.

The relevance of the interpersonal theorists to our thinking about the impact of sex-associated beliefs on interaction among women and men does not end here. As intimated by Kiesler (1983: see quote, p. 138–9), an assumption underlying the study of the interpersonal domain is that it is directly related to interpersonal behaviour. It will immediately be seen that, if this assumption is found in future to be correct, the impact of the circumplex conceptualization will be even greater.

Situation and episode perception

For the moment let us turn to recall the hypothesis, aired in chapter 3, that it might be possible to trace the genesis and perpetuation of the associations between masculinity and femininity and control and affiliation to assumptions about sex differences in activities, which could in turn be traced to assumptions about the kinds of social situations in which women and men are expected to be found. That is, men may be stereotypically associated with domains of activity that are believed to require skills related to control, while women are expected to occupy domains that require the modulation of affiliative skills.

The significance of *this* hypothesis is that it explicitly encourages us to search entirely beyond the realm of the sexual subculture to the way in which other aspects of social life contribute to the arrangement between the sexes. Is there any evidence that the constructs of control and affiliation are relevant to our general understanding of social situations and activities within them? As we shall see, the answer is a resounding 'yes'.

It is clear that much of our daily conduct is managed so as to facilitate the accomplishment of particular goals in particular situations. In general, as adults, most of us have a pretty good idea of what sorts of encounters we will have with others during a typical day, in what settings, at what times, and so on. We also have well-formed ideas about the purposes of most of these encounters, and about what kinds of conduct are permissible, desirable and likely to lead to the fulfilment of these purposes. This is not to say that we are slaves to the situations in which we find ourselves, but simply to acknowledge that the physical and social aspects of our changing environments can help us to structure our activities to satisfy goals (Smith, Giles and Hewstone, 1983).

If everyday situations are indeed structured non-arbitrarily to facilitate the achievement of interpersonal goals, then we should not be surprised to find significant parallels between the constructs that we use to order them, and the constructs that characterize the interpersonal domain in general.

In a major review of research on the impact of social context on people's thinking and behaviour, Argyle, Furnam and Graham (1981) devote a chapter to the discussion of situation-elicited goals and drives. They conclude that among the most widely recognized and salient goals of social situations are those that relate to the satisfaction of: (1) biological needs; (2) acceptance and other needs related to affiliation and approval; and (3) needs that stem from the establishment of control, over (a) the accomplishment of tasks, and (b) vertical relationships among people (dominance and status).

In their own research, for example (Graham, Argyle and Furnam, 1980), they asked students to rate the importance of each of 18 goals (selected from an earlier phase of the study to represent a broad range of very general goals, such as 'looking after own physical well-being', 'being accepted by others' and 'obtaining information') in each of several common situations (e.g. small party or gathering; complaining to a neighbour about noise). These ratings were then factor-analysed to determine relations among the perceived goals of each situation. Although the goals perceived to be most important varied from situation to situation, the factor analyses revealed three consistent groupings of goals, related to: (1) one's own well-being; (2) control (dominance, looking after others); and (3) affiliation (developing relationships, being accepted).

In related research, Forgas (1979) asked a group of housewives and a group of students to keep diaries of interaction episodes.

Later they sorted the 25 episodes most frequently mentioned by their group into categories based on their perceived similarity. Finally, they rated each episode on 12 bipolar scales. Analyses of the similarity judgements using multidimensional scaling yielded a two-dimensional solution for the housewife group. These dimensions were interpreted, with the help of the bipolar rating scales, to be related to: (1) the perceived intimacy, involvement and friendliness of the situation, and (2) the subjective self-confidence and competence of the actors. Three dimensions provided the optimal solution for the student group, related to: (1) involvement; (2) pleasantness; and (3) subjective self-confidence. It is not, I believe, stretching the interpretation of the involvement/friendliness and pleasantness dimensions to describe them as relevant to the concept of affiliation, and the self-confidence/competence dimension as relevant to control.

These studies, and many others that Forgas and Argyle *et al.* review, illustrate the salience of affiliation- and control-related concerns in encounters with others. They also illustrate that, important and recurrent as these goal dimensions may be, they are not the only ones operating. Whether the dimension 'own well-being' revealed in Graham *et al.*'s work is asymmetrically sex-associated or not, one cannot assess. In fact, there is nothing in this work explicitly to suggest the link between masculinity and control or femininity and affiliation; for this we are relying on the evidence presented earlier. At this point, the aim is simply to amass evidence that these dimensions are relevant to our thinking about the structure and dynamics of interaction in general.

A model study in this respect is reported by Wish, D'Andrade and Goodnow (1980). It builds upon earlier research in which Wish and colleagues had asked subjects to rate each of 25 common interpersonal relationships (e.g. close friends, business rivals, teammates), and self–other relationships (e.g. you and mother, you and classmates) on 25 bipolar scales. A multidimensional scaling analysis of the data indicated that four dimensions provided an optimal description of subjects' perceptions of similarities among the relationships. They were labelled: (1) co-operative and friendly *v.* competitive and hostile; (2) equal *v.* unequal; (3) intense *v.* superficial; and (4) socio-emotional and informal *v.* task-oriented and formal. Very similar dimensions were presented with 12 interpersonal relationships combined with 10 situational contexts (e.g. blaming one another for a serious error, talking to each other at a large social gathering) to form 120 hypothetical communication episodes.

Wish, D'Andrade and Goodnow (1980) were concerned to demonstrate the robustness of these findings when tested in the context of real communication. In this study, students viewed a videotape of 20 short segments of dyadic interaction, and rated the participants (40 in all) on 12 bipolar rating scales. Additional data were collected from another group of students on three dimensions of meaning from the semantic differential (active–passive; good–bad; strong–weak: Osgood, Suci and Tannenbaum, 1957) and three dimensions from Bales and Cohen's (1979) system of interaction analysis. Analysis of the data yielded four factors, accounting for about 90 per cent of the variance in descriptions of the speakers, that were strikingly similar to those obtained in the previous study. The authors concluded that the convergence of results for the studies of hypothetical and real communication and their correspondence with those of other investigators attests to their stability and generality across stimulus domains, experimental methodologies, and data analysis procedures (Wish, D'Andrade and Goodnow, 1980).

Thus, it seems that we can use the vocabulary and structure of the interpersonal domain as a shorthand for describing in part the expected impact of different situations on interpersonal behaviour. This certainly adds credibility to the idea that stereotypes about feminine and masculine interpersonal behaviour emanate from the characteristics of situations in which they are expected to be found, and activities characteristically performed within them. A more rigorous proof of this hypothesis would require a systematic attempt to discover more about sex stereotypes that cover expected differences in social activities and interests, and the characterization of these in terms of interpersonal behaviour. Additional lines of evidence will emerge below. The major virtue of establishing the links between the sexual subculture and the interpersonal domain on one hand, and the psychology of situations on the other, is that it broadens the scope of our analysis of communicative resources considerably. It forces us to consider the impact of context above and beyond sex class and gender identity on the management of interaction.

Communication Resources and Tactics

Let us pull together the main implications of the material reviewed above. Based on research in the interpersonal domain of personality, we can hypothesize that: (1) variations in the feminine aspect of gender identity will be manifest in variations in the management of interpersonal resources that are related to affiliation, while variations in the masculine aspect of gender identity will correlate with the modulation of control-related resources; and that (2) variations in the management of affiliation- and control-related resources will cause variations in their attribution to femininity and masculinity, respectively. Furthermore, to the extent that women more frequently and to a greater degree identify with the norms of femininity, and men with the norms of masculinity, we would expect that (3) women will be more preoccupied with the management of affiliation in interaction, and men more absorbed with the demands of control. Similarly, (4) women may be *expected to be* preoccupied with affiliation, and men with control thus interfering with the perception of other skills.

The research on the perception of situations would lead us to hypothesize that (5) reactions to situations that differ in ways related to control will be better predicted by masculinity than by femininity, and, conversely, reactions to situations that are normatively affiliative will be better predicted by femininity. Finally, and again only to the extent that femininity is a more central aspect of women's social identity, and masculinity of men's, (6) women will be more adept in general at interaction in affiliative contexts, and men in situations that require the exertion of control.

We now confront a most difficult task. In order to examine the hypotheses, we have to be able to specify how the interpersonal goals of interaction are realized in behaviour. How are resources managed to achieve affiliation, control or for that matter any other vector in the interpersonal domain? Much of what we know in this respect is fragmentary, and at several points we will have to rely on informed guesses about the meaning of different tactics, and the norms governing different situations.

For a model example of a procedure that researchers in this area could aspire to, we return to the study conducted by Wish, D'Andrade and Goodnow (1980), described earlier. Subsequent to obtaining viewers' impressions of the videotaped interactions, trained observers segmented the stream of communication in each episode into 'speech act units', corresponding roughly to sentences (or fragments of sentences) within speaker turns. These speech acts were then encoded into five superordinate categories (assertions, evaluations, reactions, questions and requests), each of which was further defined by subordinate categories. Eventually correlations were computed between 30 speech act variables and the factor scores from the four factors that emerged from subjects' impressions of the episodes. The factor related to the perception of control (labelled 'ascendancy' by Wish *et al.*) correlated positively with the 'percentage of acts in an episode made by the speaker', 'non-reactive assertions' (i.e. those not made in response to something previously said), 'forceful requests' and 'requests for agreement/commitment/action'. This factor correlated negatively with 'forceless assertions' and 'agreements'. The factor related to affiliation (labelled 'evaluation' in the original study) correlated positively with 'positive tension release' (e.g. laughing), 'gives attention', 'asks information' and 'answers'. The perception of affiliation correlated negatively with 'negative evaluations of hearer', 'judgemental assertions', 'disagreements', 'forceful assertions', 'gives evaluation' and 'refusals'.

Information was not presented in this study on sex differences in the use of different speech acts, or on the perception of female and male speakers. I offer it as a model primarily because the researchers made a well-organized attempt to elicit and measure the perceived dimensions of interpersonal interaction, and to relate these to a systematic description of communicative behaviours. The study is not without its problems, since we do not know how representative the interaction episodes were, or how well speech act analysis corresponds to the features of interaction that were actually significant to the naive listeners. However, these problems cannot be settled on theoretical grounds alone, and the methodology of Wish *et al.* provides a very respectable starting point for further analysis.

There is no reason in principle why the speech variables discussed in chapter 4 could not be submitted to the same kind of direct analysis. We have seen that variations in vocal, intonational, paralinguistic and perhaps phonological and grammatical variables permit inferences about speakers' masculinity and femininity frequently as they relate to interpersonal behaviour. However, the descriptive priorities of most of these studies, especially the focus on sex differences, has tended to overshadow the analysis of these resources as elements of a genuinely communicative repertoire that can be strategically exploited. We need to know more about how they are managed to indicate friendliness and to exert control.

Femininity, masculinity and communication

Even though some of the major hypotheses above are cast in terms of the communication correlates of gender identity, readers will note the conspicuous absence of reference to the constructs of femininity and masculinity throughout the review of communication resources that follows. This is due to the simple fact that most of the potentially relevant studies on this topic have been preoccupied with the communication correlates of psychological androgyny, and have therefore used instruments like the BSRI to classify subjects into Masculine, Feminine, Undifferentiated and Androgynous groups. Problems associated with the measurement tool itself and with the classification procedures adopted make it very difficult to interpret the findings within the present framework.

For example, Crosby and her colleagues (Crosby, Jose and Wong-McCarthy, 1981; Jose, Crosby and Wong-McCarthy, 1980) measured several indices of 'women's style' (Lakoff, 1975) in the speech of male–female dyads who were instructed to discuss an ethical dilemma as if they were in a class debate, or as if they were having a conversation at a party. Subjects had earlier completed the BSRI and the PAQ, and were classified as Masculine, Feminine, Androgynous or Undifferentiated. Analyses of variance according to sex, sex-role category and conversation situation revealed no significant effects, although subsequent analyses on a subsample of students who were classified the same way both on the BSRI and the PAQ (only 54 per cent) revealed a few reliable effects, generally inconsistent with our hypotheses.

The question is to what extent can we attribute the findings as being due to the impact (or absence thereof) of masculinity and femininity as opposed to the peculiarities of the BSRI and the median split classification procedure? Similar problems beset experiments on the impact of masculinity and femininity on conversational dominance and listener attentiveness (Bem, Martyna and Watson, 1976; Patton, Jasnoski and Sherchock, 1977; Putnam and McAllister, 1981), content and volume of conversation (Brown, 1981; Albrecht and Cooley, 1981; Ickes and Barnes, 1978); and self-reported tactics of social influence (Falbo, 1977), several of which have produced results that would otherwise support our hypotheses. In sum, new approaches to the measurement of MF will need to be implemented before further progress in this area is made.

Women's style and powerless speech?

More encouraging progress has been made in response to the comprehensive claims about sex differences in communicative style made by the American linguist, R. Lakoff (1973; 1975; 1977). As a consequence of social inequalities between the sexes, she argues, women have been taught to be deferential and unassertive, demeanours that she claims are expressed through a variety of linguistic variables that reflect women's place in society.

These elements typically co-occur in the speech of women, she believes, and should therefore be thought of as aspects of a coherent stylistic system that denotes, above all, deference and evasion from responsibility.

Lakoff (1977) categorizes these indices of 'women's style' under three headings. Under the first, *lexical traits,* are discussed women's specialized vocabularies (elaborated in the areas of fashion, cooking and decorating), the use of imprecise intensifiers (*so, such, divine, gorgeous*), the more frequent expression of emotions such as love and grief, avoidance of angry and hostile expressions, and the use of polite and euphemistic forms.

Under the second category of indices, *phonological traits,* she includes women's more traditional or correct pronunciation, the use of 'charming' foreign accents, and 'certain suprasegmental features that are identified as "feminine" in American speech'.

The third and final category includes indices at the level of the utterance or speech act, which she labels *syntactic–pragmatic characteristics.* Specifically, these include the use of questions with declarative functions (commonly called the tag-question form; e.g., *Dinner will be ready at six o'clock, all right?*), and hedging or deferring with the use of modal verbs (*could, should, may*), and other lexical items that indicate uncertainty (*kinda, sorta, more or less, like*).

Lakoff's claims have generated heated debate among researchers for a number of reasons. First, her arguments, both about the distribution of speech variables and about their significance as indices of deference, are based entirely, as she freely admits, on intuition and casual observation. She is aware of the danger of treating 'women's style' as if it is exclusively the prerogative of women, and writes, 'When I say that these features "characterize" women's speech, I mean that a women in this culture is expected to speak this way' (1977: 225). However, Lakoff fails to recognize fully the implications of distinguishing between sex differences and widely held stereotypes about sex differences, and makes relatively strong claims to the effect that 'women's style' is actually used by most women, and is not used by most men. This point of departure then leads her, in the tradition of sex difference research, to seek explanations for women's style in terms of other sex differences (primarily, socialization and role-differentiation), rather than in terms of how the norms that she articulates evolve, are propagated and are brought to bear on the behaviour of women and men in society.

Second, her observations, focusing as they do on the special properties of 'women's style', subtly reinforce the 'male-as-norm' assumption (see chapter 3) and detract attention from a more systematic analysis of communication that would be capable of embracing 'men's speech' as well.

On the other hand, Lakoff's writing provided a much-needed stimulus for research on male–female communication, for she was one of the first to apply the terminology of communicator style to the domain of female–male relations, provoking the development of functionalist research. The fact that she operationalized her concept of style so explicitly is also much to her credit, although we shall see that subsequent research has tended to cling rather unimaginatively to these somewhat arbitrary starting points.

The question of stylistic sex difference is for the moment of less importance than the issue of whether or not these variables are sex-stereotypical and what they indicate about speakers' interpersonal orientations. Edelsky (1976a) asked American schoolchildren (six-, eight- and eleven-year-olds) and adults to decide whether written statements containing supposedly male-typical or female-typical stylistic indices (including tag questions, intensifiers, commands, the exempletive *Damn!* and the expressions *Oh dear!* and *My goodness!*) would more likely be made by men, by women, or equally by members of each sex. The youngest subjects made very unreliable attributions of the statements, but older respondents, especially adults, assigned most of the statements to one sex or the other, in a manner consistent with the Lakoff description of women's speech. Statements containing the adjective *adorable* and the expressions *Oh dear!* and *My goodness!* were attributed to women more than 70 per cent of the time, while sentences containing *Damn* were reliably attributed to men.

In a second study, Edelsky (1976b) presented American adults with three typically masculine expressions (*Shit! Damn right!* and *I'll be damned!*) and three feminine expressions (*That's adorable! Oh dear!* and *My goodness!*) in written form, and asked the subjects to evaluate each expression on 10 bipolar rating scale items. Each item had a masculine pole (e.g. 'aggressive') and a feminine pole (e.g. 'not aggressive'), separated by seven scale points. The results show clearly that the feminine expressions are assigned ratings at the feminine poles of the rating scales, while the masculine expressions are described in terms of the masculine poles of the items.

Siegler and Siegler (1976) report a similar type of study which was conducted in two concurrent halves. Half of the subjects were asked to rate, on seven-point scales, the likelihood that each of 16 sentences was spoken by a man or by a woman. The sentences varied in assertive strength. Four were strong assertions (e.g. *Professional football is a bloodthirsty game*); four were of the tag question variety (e.g *Professional football is a bloodthirsty game, isn't it?*) and four were neutral controls (e.g. *We went to the zoo last week*). The other half of the subjects rated each sentence for the probable intelligence of its speaker, on a seven-point scale (bright–dumb).

Strong assertions were attributed significantly less often, and tag questions significantly more often, to women, with modal assertions occupying an intermediate position. Furthermore, strong assertions received the highest intelligence ratings, and tag questions were rated as least intelligent.

Thus Lakoff's hypotheses have proved to be a fruitful starting point for the discovery of stylistic indices of femininity and masculinity. Further evidence comes from two studies conducted by Kramer. In one study, Kramer (1974) had students assign sex to the speakers of isolated cartoon captions taken from magazines. The assigned sex was the same as that depicted in the unseen cartoons for more than 75 per cent of the captions. When asked to report how they had decided which sex to attribute, the students mentioned the logical, concise, businesslike and controlling nature of male captions, and the stupid, vague, emotional, confused and wordy features of the female ones. The stylistic stereotype apparently also prevails in the popular portrayal of men and women as speakers.

In another study, Kramer (1978) asked students to rate the extent to which each of 51 speech-related characteristics (e.g. loud speech, smooth speech, deep voice, good grammar) typified the average female and male speaker. On 36 of the items, males were rated differently from females. Male speech was characterized as more attention-seeking (demanding, boastful, loud, forceful), dominating, authoritarian, aggressive and frank. On the other hand, 'female speech can be summarized as friendly, gentle, enthusiastic, grammatically correct, but containing jibberish on trivial topics. Kind, correct, but unimportant' (1978: 158).

The latter study provides a strong link between masculinity and femininity and the more general themes of control and affiliation in communicator style. The substance of this link is demonstrated even more forcibly by an experiment on the effects of speech style on impression formation in a courtroom setting. Erickson *et al.* (1978) constructed two versions of a witness's key testimony. The 'powerless' version incorporated many intensifiers, hedges, hesitations, question forms and other variables from Lakoff's (1973) description of 'women's speech', while the 'powerful' version did not. They trained a male and a female actor to read both versions of the testimony keeping as many of the non-experimental features as possible constant, and then had different groups of listeners rate each of the male-spoken versions on personality trait scales, and on several other items about the credibility of the witness. In brief, the results showed that style was a more important determinant of the way the witnesses were rated than was the speaker's sex. Both male and female speakers were rated as more credible, competent, strong, active and likeable when reading the powerful version. Revealingly, the powerless version was not rated significantly more feminine on the MF item. However, this was the only scale on which the male and female actors were rated differently; the male witness was rated as more masculine than the female witness.

We now turn to consider the impact of these norms on sex differences. The results of studies seeking evidence of stylistic sex differences is inconsistent, but in sum militates against any simple equation between sex class and style. For example, Dubois and Crouch (1975) report the observation that, in a small university academic workshop where they recorded the participants' speech, of 33 instances of tag questions, *none* were spoken by women (roughly equal numbers of males and females participated). In a second study (Crouch and Dubois, 1977) they analysed material tape-recorded from university graduate seminars for the occurrence of tag questions, broken fluency, interjections, garbled sentences and semantically empty expressions (e.g. *and stuff like that; and all this; anything*). Examination of data from 50 females and 67 males showed that the use of tag questions, broken fluency, garbled sentences and empty expressions was much more characteristic of the male graduate student.

Hartmann (1976), reporting on interviews recorded with

elderly citizens of the State of Maine in the United States, notes that both male and female respondents produced tag question forms, with slightly more reported for females. Hartmann recorded speech in several academic and non-academic field contexts (including an office meeting, a women's discussion group and graduate seminars): only 20 examples of tag questions were observed, and they were produced in roughly equal proportions by speakers of each sex.

As a final citation of negative evidence, Brotherton and Penman (1977) analysed the recorded responses of 15 male and 19 female Australian students to three picture-cards from the Thematic Apperception Test. They found no significant differences between male and female subjects in terms of verbosity, the proportion of incomplete ideas expressed, or on a global rating of the 'abstractness' of the responses.

These studies, primarily of young people in university environments, should not tempt us to new generalizations, for the subjects and speech situations sampled may well be exceptional. Their value lies in their empirical approach, which makes the results susceptible to controlled replication and systematic extension in other settings. Some other studies should now be mentioned that appear to support the idea of stylistic sex differences.

It has been shown that women in Sweden (Oftedal, 1973), Brazil (Head, 1977) and the United States (Bailey and Timm, 1976) report that they use far less profanity and obscenity than men do in these countries, which is consistent with the assertion that women are more polite. Key (1975) mentions some informal studies by students which show that women use more re-duplicated adjectival forms, like *itsy-bitsy* and *teeny-weeny,* as well as more indirect adjectives, where men use adjectives with masculine connotations. Swacker (1975) found that women often prefaced definite numerical terms with adjectives of approximation (e.g. *about* six books; *around* five or six books) in a picture-describing task, while men did not.

O'Barr and Atkins (1980) report on observations of over 150 hours of courtroom testimony by women and men in which they monitored the frequency of indices of 'powerless' speech. Both women and men were found to vary widely in their use of these features, with a tendency for more women than men to have high scores. Similar results are reported by Crosby and Nyquist (1977), who scored male and female speakers for indices of 'women's language' in three different settings: laboratory conversations; interactions with police personnel in a suburban police station; and requests for information from male and female attendants at a large exposition. Females received significantly higher scores than males in the first and second situations; however, clients of *either sex* in the police station were much more hesitant and indirect than were the police personnel. In the last situation there was a non-significant tendency for the highest scores to be obtained by females interacting with a female attendant, and for the lowest scores to emerge from male–male encounters.

Thus, where differences emerge, they are generally consistent with the spirit of Lakoff's speculations, although hardly categorical. Furthermore, they appear to be strongly under the control of the particular speech situation. This is illustrated well by Brouwer, Gerritsen and De Haan (1979) and Brouwer (1982), who coded large numbers of utterances made in the process of buying train tickets in Amsterdam's Central Station for indices of 'women's language'. In neither study did the sex of the speaker significantly influence the production of diminutives, civilities or indices of linguistic insecurity. In both studies, however, the sex of the *addressee* (female *v.* male ticket-seller) influenced the expression of politeness, such that speakers were more polite to male addressees. Once again, these situation-specific results should not tempt us automatically to new generalizations, but they definitely indicate the need for systematic analyses of the interaction norms elicited in these contexts, and their impact on speech.

Dominance and conversational control?

The research on 'women's style' and 'powerless speech' stands in marked contrast to research that has emphasized the other side of the submissive–dominant contrast: namely, the exertion of active control over the processes of conversational interaction. Numerous studies of adults have found that men generally take more frequent and/or longer speaking turns than do women, especially in mixed-sex interactions. For example, Hilpert, Kramer and Clark (1975) conducted a study in which 57 female–male student dyads discussed, for ten minutes, measures to reduce theft on a university campus. Analyses of the tape-recorded conversation revealed that the male partner spoke more in 59 per cent of the dyads, a fact reflected in subjects' own perceptions on a post-discussion questionnaire: 72 per cent of the women selected the male as having been the one who talked more, as did 58 per cent of the men. Furthermore, when asked who contributed more to the decision reached by the dyad, men selected their partners equally as often as themselves, while women selected their partners (i.e., the males) more than twice as often (see also Argyle, Lalljee and Cook, 1968; Duncan and Fiske, 1977; Eakins and Eakins, 1976; Soskin and John, 1963; Strodbeck, 1951; Swacker, 1975; Wood, 1966; exceptions are reported by Hirschman, 1973, 1974; Markel, Long and Saine, 1976).

Of course, a potentially crucial factor in the Hilpert *et al.* study and many like it is the conversational setting or situation. The students were asked to participate in a discussion for the purpose of arriving at a decision, a situation clearly impregnated with control-related rather than primarily affiliative concerns. One method that has sometimes been used in an attempt to establish a non-task-oriented environment is to instruct subjects simply to 'get acquainted', a situation in which presumably norms of affiliation will become salient. I personally doubt, however, that the relatively formal and task-related norms of laboratory settings in which people are aware of being observed and recorded can ever be overridden by simple instructions (which are, after all, part of the experimental 'task'). If they cannot, then formal observational settings will always favour the display of control-related behaviours, and the apparent dominance of those for whom these settings have a facilitative effect – in this case, men.

This observation in no way detracts from the results of existing studies, some of which have been obtained in non-laboratory settings (e.g. Eakins and Eakins, 1976; Soskin and John, 1963) with similar results. But it does sensitize us to the need for an analysis of the contribution of setting to mixed-sex interaction patterns, and an attempt explicitly to sample situations that vary in ways related to affiliative goals. Such studies are essential before we can conclude with confidence that the simple contrast, dominant–submissive, captures the essence of male–female communication in our society.

These points apply equally to the many studies of the dynamics of female–male conversation in which patterns of turn-taking, pausing and interruption have been measured. In the most widely cited study of this type (Zimmerman and West, 1975) the investigators unobtrusively tape-recorded segments of 20 same-sex and 11 mixed-sex dyadic conversations in a variety of common public places. These were analysed for the presence of simultaneous speech by both parties, which were further classified into 'overlaps' (errors of intrusion, in which a speaker begins to speak at or close to a possible transition place in the current speaker's turn) and 'interruptions' (defined as violations of a speaker's turn, initiated well within the boundaries of the current turn – that is, at least one word away from a plausible transition point). In the 20 same-sex conversations, there were a total of just 7 interruptions and 22 overlaps, distributed evenly among the parties in conversation. In the 11 mixed-sex dyads, there were 48 interruptions and just 9 overlaps: 46 of the interruptions and all of the overlaps were perpetrated by men!

The authors conducted a follow-up study in more controlled surroundings (Zimmerman and West, 1978). Pairs of previously unacquainted subjects (10 same-sex, 5 mixed-sex dyads) were tape-recorded during a 12-minute 'get acquainted' conversation. The pattern of interruptions in the same-sex dyads was less symmetrical than in the previous study, with one of the two partners producing 73 per cent of the violations on average. This distribution was very similar in the mixed-sex dyads, with an important qualification: in every conversation, the male initiated more interruptions than did the female.

An interesting additional feature of this study is an analysis of the conversational consequences of interruption, both for the initiator and the recipient. Initiators tended most often to persevere with their sequestered 'turn' after the initial violation, regardless of sex. Male initiators, however, 'dropped out' (i.e. ceased speaking before completing the utterance) at twice the rate of female initiators. Futhermore, female recipients contested male-initiated interruptions at twice the rate of male recipients. These findings make it difficult to attribute the greater rate of male-initiated interruptions to mere submissiveness on the part of women.

What the second study gained in experimental control it may have lost in terms of the variety of situations sampled, and hence the heterogeneity of conversational goals. Nevertheless, the consistent pattern of interruptions discovered is extremely provocative, and has been oft-quoted in support of the male-dominance hypothesis. However, Aleguire (1978) warns that interruptions can serve support as well as control functions, such as enthusiastic assent, elaboration of the other person's theme and participation in the ongoing topic. This would indicate that a more specific functional analysis of interruption is required in order to see how the tactic is actually employed and perceived in mixed-sex (and same-sex) conversation. Furthermore, the focus on dominance behaviour has led to a general neglect of nurturant and supportive activity.

Results from other studies indicate that this is an important oversight. In a very detailed study of non-verbal behaviour in face-to-face interaction, Duncan and Fiske (1977) analysed several minutes of laboratory conversation between same-sex and mixed-sex dyads on 49 variables related to speech, gaze and gesture. Statistically significant sex differences emerged on many of these. For example, men took longer speaking turns, and had a greater rate of filled pauses (self-initiated pauses in the flow of an utterance that are filled with vocalizations, such as *ah, um,* etc.) than women. However, women smiled more often and for longer durations. They also laughed more often and directed their gaze for longer durations at their partners. These ancillary behaviours certainly seem to be nurturant and affiliative, although we would require the corroboration of observers and participants before being confident.

Other suggestive evidence comes from a study by Leet-Pellegrini (1980), in which same- and mixed-sex dyads discussed recommendations for improving the quality of television programming. Furthermore, in half of the dyads one member was given some task-relevant information to ponder prior to the discussion, thereby making them 'experts'. Portions of the discussions were analysed for quantity of speech, terms of assent (*yeah, right, that's true,* etc.) and other so-called supportive utterances. Participants and independent judges also rated their participation on scales related to conversational control, but unfortunately not on scales related to support and nurturance.

Interestingly, the sex of the interactant was not, in itself, a major determinant of speech behaviour or perception. Expertise, however, was: experts talked more. More importantly, the conferral of expertise upon males resulted in a pattern different from that of female experts: male experts talked more, assented and supported less than female experts, whose scores were closer to those of the non-experts. Of particular note were the scores of female experts in discussion with male non-experts, in which the females were perceived to be less dominant and in control than the males, despite their expertise. By comparison with the females, male experts appear to have sacrificed what little there was in the way of affiliative activity in this setting to the ends of control.

The results of these latter studies indicate the simultaneous presence of control- and affiliation-related activity even in these task-related environments, activity that is furthermore unevenly distributed between the sexes, and strongly influenced by situational variables. Leet-Pellegrini found that this distribution was affected more by differences in 'expertise' than by sex itself, although the interaction between sex and expertise favoured, as we would predict, the expression of supportive activity by women and assertive activity by men.

Complex considerations such as these have provided crucial insights into the interpretation of interaction patterns in two important non-experimental domains: domestic and academic. Fishman (1978, 1980) analysed tape-recordings of natural conversations from the homes of three middle-class couples, in which she found that the women, consistent with Lakoff's hypotheses, asked questions more frequently than the men, and said *you know* five times more often. However, rather than taking this as evidence of feminine insecurity, Fishman argues that the women she observed were shouldered with the responsibility for generating interaction within the home, and that they used these conversational tactics in the pursuit of this goal (see also Kramarae, 1981: chapter 9).

Treichler and Kramarae (1983) review research on women's speech, classroom interaction and the perception of communication goals and activities in academic settings. They conclude that most such contexts, with their emphasis on information, control and vertical hierarchies among participants, are more suited to the skills of men in general than to the skills of women. An exception, they argue, may be found in the structure and method of some women's studies classes, in which interaction is explicitly designed to be egalitarian and to encourage the special talents and resources of women as communicators.

The conclusions were generally supported in an analysis of perceptions of classroom experience given by 19 participants of a postgraduate humanities seminar (Treichler and Kramarae, 1983). Information obtained from structured and unstructured interviews, and a questionnaire, revealed that female students were more interested than men in goals related to interpersonal support and collaboration, both among students and between teachers and students. Male students reported being more interested in goals related to the non-personal aspects of the course (such as content), and more concerned with their own individual participation and the teacher's organization of class content. These situational analyses are consistent with our earlier hypotheses (see also Ruble and Higgins, 1976).

Persuasion and social influence

Several studies have gone beyond the description and evaluation of the kinds of conversational activities discussed above, to obtain measures of their impact on persuasion and attitude change, the favourite topics of those who are interested in how control is established. Other experimental investigations have shown that this perception can be altered significantly by additional situational variables. Bradley (1980) found that both female and male discussants were more influential in small discussion groups when they were believed to have background experience relevant to the discussion topic than when they were not. Furthermore, sex and expertise interacted in such a way that non-expert females elicited significantly more dominance and hostility, and less reasonableness, from other group members compared with expert females, and compared with males irrespective of expertise. A second experiment (Bradley, 1981) varied the sex of the speaker, the use of supportive arguments and the use of qualifiers (tag questions and disclaimers) in another laboratory study of small-group decision-making. Here, female speakers who either failed to use supportive arguments or who used qualifiers in their speech were inordinately penalized, being rated as less intelligent, less knowledgeable and less influential than female speakers who supported their arguments or did not use qualifiers, or males irrespective of their tactics.

These results indicate that, in control-related settings, men are expected to be skilful, and are consequently perceived so to be, regardless of the tactics they actually employ (at least, within the narrow range of activities studied). Women, on the other hand, are not expected to be as skilful, and thus are not perceived so to be, unless they make explicit attempts to display control-related resources (see also Roger and Schumacher, 1984; Stake and Stake, 1976). It is a pity that we do not have results from similar studies in settings less explicitly linked to assertiveness and dominance.

Content and topic

Early studies of sidewalk conversations in New York City, Columbus, Ohio, and London, England, showed that men talked to each other about money, business, amusement and other men, while female conversations were about men, clothes and other women (Landis, 1927; Landis and Burtt, 1924; Moore, 1922). In mixed-sex conversations in the United States, women appeared more often to converge to masculine topics, while in England the men adapted to the women to a certain extent (Landis, 1927).

Barron (1971) recorded samples of teachers' and pupils' classroom discussions, and analysed noun phrases according to grammatical case, which gives roughly the semantic domain and use of the noun. Females, she found, produced more participative and purposive cases, ostensibly indicating a more internally oriented and functional approach to conversation.

Males produced cases (instrumental, source and objective) showing an orientation towards objects and actions.

The method of case analysis is dubious from a social psychological point of view, since the assignment of categories to phrases, and of meaning to categories of grammatical case, is done on a largely intuitive basis. A more reliable study of sex differences in style is Aries's (1976) detailed examination of the conversations of small mixed- and same-sex groups of university undergraduates who met over five 90-minute sessions to 'get to know each other'. Not only the content, but also the whole style of the same-sex and mixed-sex groups differed. The male groups were characterized by stable dominance hierarchies wherein a few men did most of the talking, which centred around the content categories of 'competition and teasing', 'sports', 'physical aggression' and 'doing things'. In the female groups, dominance hierarchies were not so prominent a feature, and members directed much of their comment to the group as a whole instead of to a single listener. Their talk was distinguished by the categories of 'self', 'feelings', 'affiliation with others', 'home' and 'family'. In mixed-sex groups, men both initiated and received more communication, although the sexes seemed to compromise somewhat in terms of topics; the men spoke less of competition and physical aggression, the women less of home and family, and more discussion was about the group itself.

Self-disclosure

A topic of considerable importance in a great variety of interactions is oneself, and the antecedents and consequences of talk about the self have been subjects of intensive research (Chelune, 1979; Jourard, 1971). Self-disclosure consists of the voluntary revelation of personal information, which can of course relate to any aspect of the self (although the broad categories of descriptive v. evaluative disclosures have been adopted by some researchers: Morton, 1978), and serve a variety of functions (Derlega and Grzelak, 1979, propose the following: self-expression; self-clarification; social validation; relationship development; and social control).

Ideally, we should like to know how the contents and functions of self-disclosure are affected by sex class, gender identity and situational norms. While at present we are far from this ideal, some important beginnings have been made (for a review, see Archer, 1979). Generally, women report that they disclose more than men do on a standard self-report measure, and have been observed to do so in counselling interviews (e.g. Fuller, 1960; but see also Hill, 1975). In a study of self-disclosure among heterosexual and homosexual college students, Bender, Davis and Glover (1976) obtained significant correlations between self-reported self-disclosure and femininity, as measured by both the BSRI and the PAQ. As for situational influences, Brooks (1974) discovered, in a counselling-analogue situation, that any interviewer–subject pair containing a female resulted in higher subject self-disclosure. Furthermore, interviewer status was also manipulated, with the consequence that women disclosed more to lower-status interviewers, while the opposite pattern was obtained for men.

In most theoretical discussions, self-disclosure is related to intimacy and interpersonal attraction, themes that denote affiliation. If we are prepared to accept that norms of affiliation were operative in the studies described, then the results are certainly consistent with our general hypotheses.

An experiment conducted by Davis (1978) illustrates the effect of injecting the opportunity for explicit control over self-disclosure in mixed-sex interaction. Davis studied male–female interactions among British university undergraduates, in an experimental study of acquaintance formation. Members of each dyad had to take turns disclosing something about themselves, choosing from a list of topics that had previously been scaled along a continuum from low to high intimacy. Davis writes:

The results indicated that males were the principal architects of such encounters, regardless of which partner took the first turn. They proceeded independently in their choice of topics, dictating the pace at which intimacy increased during the exercise, whereas females enabled a degree of consensus to emerge by matching the pace set . . . The data are seen as consistent with traditional sex role stereotypes bearing on the control of interpersonal relationships. [p. 684]

Interpersonal conflict resolution

The final communication topic that will be discussed here is conflict resolution. Frost (1977), for example, asked students to describe the methods that they used in arguments and disputes. Women reported that they prefer to avoid confrontation, whereas men report the use of assertive tactics such as talkativeness and interruption.

Sex-related patterns of conflict management have been studied experimentally using a technique devised by Blakar (1973), in which two persons are each given a map of a relatively complicated network of streets depicting a town centre. One member of the dyad, designated the 'explainer', has two routes marked on the map, one relatively short and simple, the other longer and more complicated. No routes are marked on the map of the other member, who is called the 'follower'. The task is for the explainer to lead the follower successfully along the marked routes using only verbal instructions, first along the simple route, and then along the complicated one. The follower may ask questions, ask the explainer to repeat instructions, and so on. Herein lies the rub – the maps are not identical: they differ by one street, so that success on the complicated route is impossible (although the simple route is not affected).

Pedersen (1980) collected observations of 12 same-sex and 12 mixed-sex dyads in this situation (the female was designated explainer in half of the mixed-sex dyads, and the male in the other half), recording the number of solvers and the time taken to reach a solution by each dyad on each of the two (simple and complicated) routes.

Before examining the results of this experiment, let us consider what we might expect to find. Although the overall situation is clearly control-related, the skills required of explainer and follower differ considerably. In the simple situation, the combined efforts of an assertive explainer and a sensitive listener would be expected to facilitate efficiency, a combination favouring males in the role of explainer, and females as followers. The skills required in the conflict task, however, are different: they require the location of an incompatibility between maps (this was the criterion of conflict resolution adopted by Pedersen), which implies an assertive role on behalf of both parties, a situation favouring male–male dyads, and disfavouring asymmetrical assertive–sensitive dyads.

The results generally confirm these expectations. On the simple task all dyads managed to solve the problem successfully; males were clearly more efficient as explainers (mean time in dyads with men as explainers was 2 min. 47 sec. as compared with 4 min. 44 sec. for female explainer dyads), and females as followers (2 min. 36 sec. for female follower dyads and 4 min. 50 sec. for male follower dyads); and the fastest dyads overall were the male–female pairs, while the slowest were the female–male pairs. In the conflict situation, only 16 dyads achieved a solution (namely, consensus on the nature and location of map discrepancies) within the 40 minutes allocated. The distribution of solvers did not distinguish among dyad types, but the time required among solvers to reach a solution did: female explainer dyads took an average of 22 min. irrespective of follower sex; male–male dyads took an average of 8 min. less, and male–female dyads took 8 min. longer.

It should be emphasized that the goals of interaction, the nature of the conflict and the criteria of success in this experiment were set by the experimenter, and were held constant for all subjects. Thus, the experiment is illuminating with respect to the resolution of conflict within control-related environments where both participants are working towards the same goal. But it leaves unexplored the whole topic of conflict over the negotiation of goals themselves, how it arises and how it is managed in interaction, a topic to which we shall return later in the chapter.

The list of resources that could be analysed in this manner is potentially endless, although, as we have seen, an inordinate amount of effort has gone into the analysis of the correlates of dominance–submissiveness. In spite of this, the evidence converges to support our earlier hypotheses about the combined impact of gender identity (approximated by sex class) and situation on the management of interpersonal communication: the modulation of affiliative resources is correlated with femininity and the perception of femininity while the modulation of control-related resources is correlated with masculinity and the perception of masculinity.

Let us be clear: it is not that men are unilaterally dominant and women unilaterally affiliative – nothing so stark and categorical has been demonstrated. Neither is it that femininity is perfectly correlated with affiliation and masculinity with dominance. It is simply that masculinity tends to be expressed in terms of control-related skills, and femininity in terms of affiliation. When we consider that gender identity is a matter of degree, with large individual differences in both femininity and masculinity, the consequences of our observations for the overall arrangement between the sexes become considerably less clear-cut than most bipolar (powerful–powerless; dominant–muted) contrasts imply.

This does not, however, mean that there are *no* overall consequences. As long as we can safely assume that women are more feminine than men overall, and men more masculine than women, and as long as these gender formulae are asymmetrically correlated with norms of control and affiliation, then women and men will assume asymmetrical communicative roles, on average. We have seen some of the consequences of such asymmetries in the work reviewed above. The control-oriented person is seen as more powerful, dominant, competent, credible and persuasive. We know that the person who uses low-control resources is seen to have less of all these qualities — *but* low control does not imply high affiliation: the two dimensions are uncorrelated. Someone who is affiliation-oriented is presumably seen as warm, likeable, concerned for others, sensitive and emotional, qualities that may confer power in their own right. As yet, however, we know less about the rewards of nurturance than we do about the penalties of submissiveness.

From Tactics to Goals

To have reached some tentative conclusions regarding the impact of the sexual subculture on the management of resources and tactics in interpersonal communication is a significant achievement, especially in so far as they suggest that our conduct as members of different social categories may be closely tied to the kind of situations in which we most often find ourselves. At this point we cannot infer that one *causes* the other – it is just as plausible to assume that we engineer our lives so as to occupy situations in which we can be skilful as it is to assume that our skills are determined by the situations that we occupy.

Recall, though, that the analysis of resources and tactics is not an end in itself, but was undertaken as a means of discovering whether differences in the relative salience of interpersonal goals are manifest in patterns of resource management. The answer appears to be 'yes', although the evidence is indirect. The inference from behaviour to underlying goal structure suggested by all this work requires direct confirmation in future studies.

Furthermore, none of this work has explicitly examined the process of goal-setting itself. In most of the studies, the goals of interaction have been set by the experimenter, via instructions and choice of task, leaving participants to negotiate the method of achieving them. Given these constraints, we have seen that tactics vary as a complex function of situational norms, sex class and, presumably, gender identity. We must, however, assume that sometimes, perhaps very often, it is not the methods of achieving well-defined goals that are at issue, but the very goals of interaction themselves. The literature reviewed above lends itself rather well to the interpretation that the relative prominence of different goals varies systematically – not only within situations, but also across situations generally – with masculinity and femininity. If valid, this inference leads to an important and novel set of predictions concerning conflict and satisfaction in interpersonal relations in general, but especially in marital and other long-term mixed-sex relationships.

We have already considered the possibility that harmonious communication is constrained by the need for compatibility between (1) the implicit demands of the situations in which people characteristically find themselves, and (2) the skills of resource management that interactants characteristically exercise. Different combinations of skills seem optimal in different situations, and it should be possible to predict, within limits, the combination of skills most conducive to smooth interaction among couples subject to the stresses of different environments. If, however, these skills can be read as the expression of tactics motivated by the desire to achieve specific goals – that is, not just as fixed states of being, but as manifestations of goal-directed tendencies – then we must add another term to the formula for predicting satisfactory interpersonal interaction. It might be hypothesized that, almost independently of the fit between the demands of situations and the tactics of resource management employed by the participants, feelings of success and satisfaction will depend on the degree to which a relationship provides opportunities for the achievement of each participant's goals.

I am suggesting that femininity and masculinity are more than just static elements in the structure of social identity, that they are projects taken up in the pursuit of security. As such, they will be manifest in both the characteristic base-rate or start-up levels of masculinity- and femininity-related tactics, and attempts to transform the relationship in a direction that is congruent with the dominant objective of a person's identity project. I would furthermore suggest that few people are consumed with such a singleminded clarity of purpose that the goals of either femininity or masculinity will be pursued to the total exclusion of the other. The question to be answered is whether or not it is possible to predict the relative urgency of masculinity- and femininity-related goals, and hence the pressure towards attaining them, and tolerance for other people's identity projects. A base-rate measure of femininity and masculinity such as those discussed and employed in chapters 5 and 6 would probably not suffice, because we require a measure not only of gender identity, but also of the security of identity. Such a measure has yet to be devised.

On an even more speculative note, I will suggest that the net effect of asymmetrically distributed interpersonal goals may be that men more often tend to control the process and outcome of interaction, while women attempt to manage affiliative goals within the domains of interaction that are prescribed by men. In effect, the interactants in mixed-sex encounters may sometimes be negotiating at cross-purposes, resulting in misunderstanding, conflict and dissatisfaction. Difficult problems arise when this conflict becomes the focus of interaction. Unless and until it is recognized that the root of the conflict lies in differences of interactional purpose, interactants may attempt to accommodate to each other by changing levels of control or affiliation without converging in terms of underlying goals. On the other hand, people may find that converging in terms of goals is unsatisfactory because it necessitaties the abandonment of the original salient and satisfying goal-dimension. For example, women may acquire the skills of assertiveness and thus successfully engage in control-related aspects of interaction, while still feeling that they have not solved the essential problem of goal divergence, or satisfied the affiliative requirements of interaction.

This raises two final issues that merit further attention. The first is the question of repertoire. At many points in this chapter I have used terms (such as 'skill') that intimate that patterns of resource management are manifestations not simply of choice, but of an underlying resource base or repertoire. The implication is that one's social identity may influence the skills that one acquires as well as the skills that one chooses to employ. This has not been proven, but it is an implicit background assumption of programmes that seek to resolve communication problems through skills-training. This raises the possibility that inter-personal convergence, even at the level of tactics of resource management, let alone at the level of goals, may be problematic for people who have limited repertoires. The influence of gender identity on communicative repertoire, and its implications for interpersonal relations, urgently require study.

So also do the dynamics of goal-setting and resource management in on-going same-sex and mixed-sex interactions: we need to know not just about start-up and base-rate levels of control and affiliation, but also about how they change and to what effect. Future research will, I hope, contribute to the resolution of these issues.

8

Language, the Sexes and Social Change

Social Conflict and Patterns of Response

The hypothesis of a sexual subculture, a distinctive domain of thought and activity devolving upon the criteria for sex classification and the subsequent implications for men and women, appears to be unassailable in our society, and perhaps in all societies. These are preoccupations that profoundly influence every human being and make it meaningful to write of female–male relations in the terms adopted in this book. This does not imply that the arrangement between the sexes is predicated on consensus, however, and almost every detail of this arrangement has been subject to scrutiny and criticism, especially since the advent of modern feminism in the past 15–20 years. The aim of this chapter is to isolate some of the more salient sources of language-related social conflict in female–male relations, and to illustrate strategies for resolving them.

The most obvious sources of feminist discontent arise from asymmetries and prejudices in social representation outlined in chapter 3. The misrepresentation and under-representation of women in reference materials and in the media, in practices of naming and address, in patterns of nominal and pronominal reference and in the proliferation of stereotypes and prejudices via the metaphorical thematization of female–male relations have all come in for extended criticism (e.g. Nilsen *et al.*, 1977). Feminine and masculine speech, or, more specifically, evaluations of feminine and masculine speech, have also been the focus of critiques and recommendations for change, as have aspects of sex-associated interaction strategies. Finally, it has even been argued that the resources of communication themselves are products of male culture, and furthermore that men have prevented women from actively participating in the creation and development of language (Spender, 1980).

It hardly needs pointing out that the impetus to critiques of the role of language in relations between the sexes is the fact that asymmetries in social representation, the evaluation of speech style, interaction management and access to resources generally converge with data from other sources indicating that women as a group are accorded a lower status than men. I have indicated how I believe the study of language can contribute to our understanding of the texture and dynamics of female–male differentiation, at once both broadening and sharpening our analysis of the sexual subculture. I have derided the sex difference fetish, shown that perceptions of femininity as well as of masculinity can have beneficial consequences in some and possibly many contexts, and called for an analysis of interaction that takes account of nurturance as well as dominance.

None of these considerations, however, leads me to question the conclusion drawn on the basis of so much evidence, that women as a class stand at a distinct and pervasive social disadvantage to men in our society, not just in reputation, but in fact (e.g. Reid and Wormald, 1982). I also believe that the desiderata for this conclusion must continue to be debated in order to expand our understanding of the mechanisms of social differentiation. A personal commitment to this point of view is not a necessary prerequisite to identifying the sources of conflict and their consequences, however.

The feminist interpretation of women's status in society, to the extent that it casts women in a comparatively unfavourable light, entails the recognition of a direct and transparent threat to the security of women's social identity. Recall from chapter 6 that security is the degree to which one's awareness of group membership contributes positively and reliably to one's self-concept. A basic assumption of almost every major theory of social behaviour (cf. Shaw and Constanzo, 1982; Turner, 1982) is that people are motivated to maintain positive self-evaluations and thus react to threats in predictable ways. The discussion that follows is based in part on a model of reactions to negative social identity proposed by Tajfel and his colleagues (Tajfel, 1978a, b; Tajfel and Turner, 1979; Williams and Giles, 1978).

First, we must recognize that people may respond to inferior status with either acceptance or rejection. Acceptance will predominate among those who do not perceive alternatives to the current status quo. Economic, political and psychological factors that contribute to the awareness of such alternatives will lead to patterns of rejection. Tajfel intimates that one can become aware of alternatives to the status arrangement itself, or to the system of values on which it is based, or both, or neither, that is, one can respond with acceptance or rejection to either or both of these aspects of the status quo. These two distinctions (acceptance *v.* rejection; status arrangement *v.* value system) combine to yield the four major categories of response to inferiority depicted in table 8.1. Additionally, within each category, one can distinguish between individual and group responses. Individual responses are based on attempts to change the relation between oneself and one's group, while group strategies are attempts to change one's whole group. Labels have been attached to various patterns of response in table 8.1, which will be elaborated upon below.

Table 8.1 Reactions to inferior group status

	Accept status	*Reject status*
Accept value system:	Individual: Self-hate	Individual: Mobility Disidentification
	Group: Resignation	Group: Assimilation Competition
Reject value system:	Individual: Withdrawal Therapy	Individual: Anomie
	Group: Reform	Group: Conflict Creativity

Acceptance and Rejection

Most of the activity of the women's movement is devoted to stimulating awareness of alternatives to the subtractive aspects of female–male relations, as a means of facilitating and encouraging social change. Patterns of acceptance are therefore not usually discussed in detail by feminist authors writing about language, who comprise the majority of authoritative figures in the area. Most expositions consist of descriptions and explanations of the status quo, and recommendations for change. Thus we may overlook the fact that patterns of acceptance are precisely the status quo that fuel feminist scholarship, research and polemic. As such, major correlates of acceptance can be inferred from the data that have been described in previous chapters. The most recurrent theme of these chapters has been that accepted descriptions and interpretations of these patterns require further elaboration before we can be completely confident as to their significance in the lives of women and men. Nevertheless, the psychological and behavioural correlates of acceptance as they will be described do seem applicable to at least some women.

A classic pattern of individual response to the acceptance of both inferior status and its underlying value system is the phenomenon of so-called *self-hate,* of which examples abound in the context of relations between ethnic groups. Feelings of embarrassment and shame at one's social identity have at various points in history been characteristic of members of many racial and ethnolinguistic groups (Giles, 1978, 1979; Milner, 1981). One might speculate that such reactions would be manifest in terms of public hesitancy and silence, apology and other forms of overt deference and submissiveness (which, it must be recalled, is different from the expression of nurturance and affiliation), features that figure prominently in many accounts of so-called 'women's speech'.

This individual response may be accompanied by attempts from other group members to engender the acquiescence of the whole group to its inferior role. This strategy of *resignation* is sometimes advocated in traditionalist reactions to modern feminism, and, while it does not necessitate self-hate, it nevertheless poses advocates with the difficult problem of reconciling the negative consequences of an admittedly second-rate status.

Myths of heroes and champions notwithstanding, history warns that human misery does not spontaneously generate the seeds of its own destruction; and, despite the fact that acceptance of the type described above does little to ameliorate negative social identity, the transition from acceptance to rejection is not automatic. A detailed analysis of the social conditions that have led to the emergence of awareness in alternatives to the status quo is unfortunately beyond the author's competence; however, it is clear that many such alternatives exist today. On the one hand, the perception of instability in the system of androcentrism has led to the rejection of the status arrangement itself among many people, while assaults on the legitimacy of the value system underpinning male–female relations have led to criticism and rejection of this aspect of the arrangement.

Before turning to these patterns and their consequences, let us draw attention to the vital role of communication and social influence in mediating the awareness of alternatives, especially in the development of group responses. This is where the feminist movement as a whole has had its greatest impact to date: in the articulation and interpretation of female experience, in the creation of forums where these can be shared and debated, and in the formulation of responses to the status quo.

Individuals who for whatever reason accept the position of inferiority, but reject the value system on which it is predicated, might be expected to react by *withdrawing* from participation in mainstream culture. This would result in avoidance of public contexts, and an apparent loss of voice, or mutedness. This too is a prominent theme in descriptions of the female role in the sexual subculture, as we have seen. The comparable group response would consist of collective withdrawal, perhaps combined with attempts to establish new, non-comparative bases for group identification. Tajfel points to the example of Jewish *shtetls,* small insular communities in Russia and eastern Europe at the turn of the century that provided Jews with a sense of community while enabling them to withdraw from contexts of persecution. Such a collective withdrawal would not at first glance appear to constitute a realistic alternative for most women, although the establishment of feminist communes and some forms of radical lesbianism qualify in this category. Another form of individual response of this type may consist of psychotherapy, sought in the attempt to reconcile problems arising from the discrepancy between one's values and one's status. The implications of this response as far as language is concerned are vague.

A final and important pattern at this level is the collective call to *reform the value system,* which is a preferred strategy among many feminists. The call to reform values does not in itself entail any change of practice, but is based on the belief that practices will change as a consequence of shifts in attitude. Reform is usually only one of several planks in the platform of most popular feminist movements.

It will be seen that the responses described above do not in themselves go far to change the status arrangement that is the stimulus for conflict. The third major category of response is characterized by the rejection of the status arrangement and the simultaneous acceptance of the underlying value system, which may occasionally lead to more successful resolutions, although probably not often. At the individual level, for example, this pattern is manifest by someone who attempts to dis-identify with the original group, and to acquire the characteristics and behaviours that would allow her to 'pass', or *mobilize,* into the group with higher status. The comparable group strategy is the collective attempt to lose features that distinguish the low-status group and acquire valued characteristics of the 'superior' group. In ethnic group relations, especially between groups without visible markers, the strategy of *assimilation* may sometimes be successful, although at the cost of whatever may have been valued about the original group.

There are obvious limitations to the effectiveness of these strategies in the sexual subculture, however, given the nature of the criteria that are the foundation of the female–male distinction. Of course, many of the less central criteria, including those embracing speech and communication, are mutable, and one could argue that, even though complete assimilation may not be feasible, any strategy that reduces differences between the low- and high-status groups will alleviate the negative consequences of between-group comparisons for those of lower status. This is the kind of thinking that has fuelled those elements of feminist theory that advocate the abandonment of all that is feminine in favour of the wholesale adoption of characteristics and behaviours identified as masculine, including patterns of speech and communication. From this point of view, responses that encourage women as a group to acquire the elements of a traditionally masculine repertoire – assertiveness training, for example – and to avoid the expression of nurturance and emotion might be regarded as examples of assimilationism.

They might also be regarded as examples of outright *competition* with the dominant group for resources and characteristics that confer prestige according to the present value system. Conflicts over scarce resources are of course characteristic of relations between many kinds of groups, and another main plank in the platform of modern feminism is the desire to achieve equality for women in traditionally valued domains of society. As far as language goes, this means equal access to resources and positions of authority in the media and other contexts of public communication, the acquisition of skills necessary to exert influence in the traditionally male-dominated domains of higher education and politics, not to mention industry, the church and the military. It also entails equal rights before the law, rights that have in the past been debated on the point of whether 'women' are to be included in the category 'persons' for legal purposes (see Land, 1978; Sachs and Wilson, 1978).

Of course, advocates of competitive strategies are seldom interested exclusively in changes of status relations; such changes are often viewed as a prerequisite to achieving a reorganization of social values. This brings us to the final category of responses to inferior status: rejection of both the arrangement and the value system. If adopted as an individual response, this pattern of double rejection may result in the classic problems of alienation and *anomie* – individuals become isolated from their own group as a consequence of disidentification, and from the potential rewards of membership in the high-status group as a consequence of rejecting the values that make them superior. As a collective strategy, however, based upon co-ordinated activity on behalf of the group as a whole, the individual need not suffer from the feeling of isolation, although this does not imply that collective patterns of double rejection are necessarily more successful than are calls to reform, or competitive responses.

Most contemporary challenges to the status quo are based on

patterns in this category. In the domain of language, at least as far as social representation goes, these have been remarkably successful, having resulted in the adoption of official guidelines for the improvement of the image of women and the use of non-sexist language in textbooks and dictionaries by many publishing houses and official organizations (*Guidelines for Improving the Image of Women*, 1972; *Guidelines for Equal Treatment of the Sexes,* 1972; American Psychological Association, 1975). The most straightforward pattern of response in this category we will simply call *conflict*, the tenor of which can be inferred from guidelines that have been adopted as a direct consequence of feminist protest. The US National Council for Teachers of English (NCTE) in 1975, for example, adopted a comprehensive set of recommendations for the use of nonsexist language in the organization's publications and correspondence (Nilsen *et al.,* 1977). Under the heading 'General Problems' are detailed recommendations for dealing with the issues of (1) the omission of women, (2) demeaning women, and (3) sex-role stereotyping. Regarding the first of these issues, the NCTE recommends avoiding the generic use of *man* and its compounds in any context where the referent could be either female or male. The diminution of women can be avoided by referring to women and men in a parallel manner in descriptions of jobs, appearance, and marital status, and by avoiding terms that trivialize women (such as *gal Friday* and *Women's Libber*). The elimination of sex-role stereotyping can be facilitated by showing women participating equally with men in contexts where they appear together, and by avoiding the implicit association of jobs and other roles exclusively with one sex or the other. Moving on to 'Specific Issues', the guidelines suggest procedures to follow in order to reduce sexism in books and edited collections, in booklist selections, teaching units, research and journal articles.

The existence of these formal statements, and the influence that they have had on both language use and the awareness of issues, is impressive testimony to the power of the collective voice to affect social change. It should be borne in mind however that language change of this nature does not in itself guarantee the accomplishment of social change in other aspects of the arrangement between the sexes. The hope is that, as one element in a programme of action, it contributes no less than changes in employment practices, legal rights, patterns of domestic activity and so on.

Another pattern of rejection in this category has been termed *social creativity,* and encompasses tactics designed to result in status and value changes by means of either the redefinition of hitherto negatively valued characteristics, or the creation of entirely new bases for social identity, or both. These patterns usually accompany conflict responses. Taking redefinition first, classic examples consist in re-evaluations among American blacks during the 1960s and 1970s of previously stigmatizing characteristics, including skin colour, fashion, food and music. Among women, emphasis on the value of emotional expression, affiliation, domestic labour and other stereotypically feminine resources and styles are evident, even to the extent of successfully encouraging men to acquire these skills.

Turning to the creation of new dimensions of evaluation, we may consider the effect of changes in naming practices, whereby women are more frequently retaining their family names when they marry, thus indicating new pride in matrilineal heritage. The adoption of the address form, *Ms* by many women may constitute another example, although I suspect that there are a variety of individual as well as group motives for this change, not all of which are predicated on conflict. It is conceivable that some women perceive this as a tactic of individual mobility or of assimilation.

A taxonomy such as this depends upon extremes for the purpose of illustration and example. It may be difficult to find individuals or organizations that respond in one and only one of the patterns described above, and most women probably react to the status quo in different ways at different times, depending on the strategies that suit their needs and predicaments. There are, besides, undoubtedly patterns of response that I have overlooked. The important point is that it is eminently feasible systematically to describe patterns of response to arrangements between the sexes, to chart the implications of these patterns for individual and social change, and ultimately to explain the transition from patterns of acceptance to rejection. As to the factors that contribute to this transition, and to the effectiveness of the resulting responses in resolving the negative consequences of inferior status, these are questions for further research.

Reactions to Rejection

I do not wish to convey the mistaken impression that, were it not for modern feminism, the status quo would prevail in a state of equilibrium. For one thing, the rejection of androcentrism has a long, largely unwritten history (Rowbotham, 1973; Spender, 1983), and the relative status of women has been in flux probably since the dawn of civilization and culture. For another thing, social change does not necessarily imply overturning the status quo – change can also be exerted in the direction of consolidating the inequities of existing arrangements. While the success of such tendencies appears to be on the wane in contemporary Western societies, the resurgence of religious fundamentalism and other factors in many parts of the world have produced exactly the opposite effect, and women have lost at a swoop liberties and rights won only after decades of persistent struggle.

Furthermore, not all men are content with an arrangement that implies superiority and security of identity for their kind at the expense of women as a class. One does not have to be a woman to be an active feminist, and many men have found good reasons to pursue strategies of change in support of women. Just as not all women are feminists, so not all men are reactionary.

These sensibilities notwithstanding, the main trend of social change in the arrangement between the sexes in our society is towards equality for women, and the main thrust of this movement has been and will continue to be carried by women. Nevertheless, while the onus of the pressure towards change is borne primarily by those who stand to gain from it, the ultimate success of these endeavours will depend in part on the reactions of those who stand (or perceive that they stand) to lose.

Patterns of acceptance on behalf of women do not pose threats to supremacist men, and thus do not call for explicit reaction beyond perhaps encouragement, support and shoring up cracks in the walls of perceived legitimacy and stabililty. Moves to reject the value system and the status arrangement, however, will be met with predictable patterns of resistance.

A greater variety of language-related response is discernable in reactions to challenges to the value system than in reactions to threats to the stability of the status hierarchy. The most robust of these is outright denial that an issue exists, or to label such issues as products of a deviant, probably lunatic, fringe. In its most intransigent form, this reaction asserts simply that there are no inequities in the arrangement between the sexes, either in representation or in fact, a position that precludes debate about social change and how it should be implemented. Denial is often buttressed with the tactics of obfuscation, pedantic argument and rationalization.

Blaubergs (1980) discusses several categories of argument against changing sexist language that qualify in this regard. First, there is the argument that sexist language does not exist: 'I suspect that much denunciation of sexist language in others reveals the bias of the hearer rather than the speaker' (Tavard, 1977: p. 136). This kind of denial assumes that sexism must be active and deliberate in order to be considered unfair, and that the perceptions of those most directly affected count for little or nothing. Various forms of pedantry are also brought into play in defence of the status quo. A favourite refutation of calls for sociolinguistic change is based on the premise that feminists believe that language determines sexism. Since this can easily be shown not to be true in a strict causal sense, then, goes the argument, the need for change in language practices is obviated. Of course the premise upon which the argument rests is a vulgarization of the feminist claim that language 'reflects, influences, reinforces, maintains, or otherwise facilitates the continued existence of sex-role stereotyping and sexism in societal institutions and practices' (Blaubergs, 1980), which is a perfectly adequate premise on which to base an appeal for social change.

Another argument is that preoccupations with language run the risk of either contributing an aura of triviality to the feminist cause, or diverting energy from more pressing issues. Readers of this book will be in a position to judge the merit of this line of reasoning for themselves. Rationalization is another tactic of reaction: change is too difficult, and besides, who could contemplate rewriting the library of history and literature to conform with the Newspeak of Unisex?

Whatever these arguments lack in intellectual integrity, they make up for in emotional vigour, which is illustrated even better by reactions based on derision and the use of sarcasm. In 1776 Abigail Adams wrote to her husband John Adams in America, as he and his colleagues were preparing the legal basis for American independence. She advised that the rights of women should be more generously remembered in the new code of law than they had been previously: 'If particular care and attention is not paid to the ladies, we are determined to foment a rebellion, and will not hold ourselves bounded by any laws in which we have no voice or representation.' Her husband replied,

As to your extraordinary code of laws, I cannot but laugh. We have been told that our struggle has loosened the bonds of government everywhere; that children and apprentices were disobedient; that schools and colleges were grown turbulent; that Indians slighted their guardians, and that Negroes grew insolent to their masters. But your letter was the first intimation that another tribe, more numerous and powerful than the rest, were grown discontent. [quoted in Miller and Swift, 1976: 35, 36]

Numerous modern examples are contained in Blaubergs (1980), Veitch (1981), and White and Wood (1982), the most ostentatious of which was a 1973 *New York Times* column penned by Russell Baker, from which Miller and Swift quote the following extract:

Like-person-you know! Where's your personners, person? You've been personipulating me! I must get back to serious thinking about the President's persondate, the persontle of greatness, penpersonship, oneupspersonship, the decline of the praying persontis, Persondrake and the Magician and whether the Presidency is still attainable by Governor . . . Rockefolk.

Blauberg points out that this kind of ridicule is usually based on the misapplication of reasonable proposals for sociolinguistic change – in this case, on an overextension of the proposal that the generic *man* be avoided, such that the morphemic structure of words otherwise irrelevant to the issue is violated.

Once again, in the interest of confining my discussion to topics related to language, important patterns of reaction have undoubtedly been overlooked, especially those that bear directly on challenges to the stability of the status arrangement such as division, coercion, legalism and disenfranchisement. Furthermore, I have made no attempt to ground the processes of social change and reaction in their wider economic, political and historical context in this chapter, or in any other of the book. Instead, I have dwelt on the social psychological and sociolinguistic antecedents, correlates and consequences of relations between the sexes, in order to emphasize their necessity, without asserting their priority.

There is, to be sure, much more that could be written about language, the sexes and society than I have included in this short book. I chose deliberately to concentrate on male-female relations in the English-speaking world, my aim being to apply a sociogenetic framework to the description and explanation of observations collected within one cultural context. The descriptive parameters of the arrangement between the sexes, its antecedents, correlates and consequences, are very different in other parts of the world, and discussion of language would be at best superficial without prior elucidation of these differences. Fortunately, excellent progress is being made in this area (Borker, 1980; Brown, 1980; Maltz & Borker, 1982), as well as in the application of research on language and the sexes to the solution of specific social problems (Treichler, 1984).

References

Addington, D. W. (1968). The relationship of selected vocal characteristics to personality perception. *Speech Monographs, 35* (4), 492–503.

Akinnaso, F. N. (1981). Names and naming principles in cross-cultural perspective. *Names, 29* (1), 37–63.

Albrecht, T. L. and Cooley, R. E. (1981). Androgyny and communication strategies for relational dominance: An empirical analysis. *Communication Yearbook,* vol. 4, New Brunswick, NJ: Transaction.

Aleguire, D. G. (1978). Interruptions as turn-taking. Paper presented at the International Sociological Association Ninth World Congress of Sociology, Uppsala University, Sweden.

American Psychological Association Task Force on Issues of Sexual Bias in Graduate Education (1975). Guidelines for nonsexist use of language. *American Psychologist, 30* (6), 682–4.

Anshen, F. (1969). Speech variation among Negroes in a small southern community. Unpublished PhD dissertation, New York University.

Archer, R. L. (1979). Role of personality and the social situation. In G. J. Chelune *et al.* (eds), *Self-disclosure: Origins, Patterns and Implications in Interpersonal Relations.* San Francisco: Jossey-Bass.

Argyle, M., Furnham, A. and Graham, J. A. (1981). *Social Situations.* Cambridge: Cambridge University Press.

Argyle, M., Lalljee, M. and Cook, M. (1968). The effects of visibility on interaction in a dyad. *Human Relations, 21,* 3-17.

Aries, E. (1976). Interaction patterns and themes of male, female, and mixed groups. *Small Group Behavior, 7* (1), 7–18.

Aronovitch, C. D. (1976). The voice of personality: Stereotyped judgements and their relation to voice quality and sex of speaker. *Journal of Social Psychology, 99,* 207–20.

Austin, J. L. (1962). *How to Do Things with Words*. Oxford: Oxford University Press.

Bagely, C. (1979). Self-esteem as a pivotal concept in race and ethnic relations. *Research in Race and Ethnic Relations, 1,* 127–67.

Bailey, L. A. and Timm, L. A. (1976). More on women's and men's expletives *Anthropological Linguistics, 18,* 438-49.

Bakan, D. (1966). *The Duality of Human Existence*. Chicago: Rand McNally.

Bales, R. F. and Cohen, S. P. (1979). *Systematic Multiple Level Observation of Groups*. New York: Free Press,

Barron, N. (1971). Sex-typed language: The production of grammatical cases. *Acta Sociologica, 14* (1–2), 24–72.

Bate, B. (1975). Generic man, invislble woman: Language, thought and social change. *University of Michigan Papers in Women's Studies,* 2 (1), 83–95.

Baumel, M. H. and Lewis, M. (1971). Infants' attentional distribution across two modalities. Paper presented at the meeting of the Eastern Psychological Association, New York City.

Beaucom, D. H. (1976). Independent masculinity and femininity scales on the California Psychological Inventory. *Journal of Consulting and Clinical Psychology, 44* (5), 876.

Bell, R. and Darling, J. (1965). The prone head reaction in the human newborn: Relationship with sex and tactile activity. *Child Development, 36,* 943–9.

Bem, S. L. (1974). The measurement of psychological androgyny. *Journal of Consulting and Clinical Psychology, 42* (2), 155–62.

Bem, S. L. (1977). On the utility of alternative procedures for assessing psychological androgyny. *Journal of Consulting and Clinical Psychology, 45* (2), 196–205.

Bem, S. L., Martyna, W. and Watson, C. (1976). Sex typing and androgyny: Further explorations of the expressive domain. *Journal of Personality and Social Psychology, 34,* 1016–23.

Bender, V. L., Davis, Y. and Glover, O. (1976). Patterns of self-disclosure in homosexual and heterosexual college students. *Sex Roles, 2,* 149–60.

Berko-Gleason, J. (1978). Sex differences in the language of children and parents. In O. Garnica and M. King (eds), *Language, Children and Society*. London: Pergamon Press, 149–58.

Berlin, B. and Kay, P. (1969). *Basic Color Terms: Their Universality and Evolution*. Berkeley: University of California Press.

Berzins, J. I. (1977). Therapist–patient matching. In A. S. Gurman and

A. M. Razin (eds), *Effective Psychotherapy: A Handbook of Research*. New York: Pergamon Press.

Berzins, J. I., Welling, M. A. and Wetter, R. E. (1978). A new measure of psychological androgyny based on the personality research form. *Journal of Consulting and Clinical Psychology, 46* (1), 126–38.

Bierman, R. (1969). Dimensions of interpersonal facilitation in psychotherapy and child development. *Psychological Bulletin, 723,* 338–52.

Billig, M. G. (1976). *Social Psychology and Intergroup Relations*. London: Academic Press.

Blakar, R. M. (1973). An experimental method for inquiring into communication. *European Journal of Social Psychology, 3,* 415–25.

Blaubergs, M. S. (1980). An analysis of classic arguments against changing sexist language. *Women's Studies International Quarterly, 3* (2/3), 135–47.

Bodine, A. (1975). Sex differentiation in language. In B. Thorne and N. Henley (eds), *Language and Sex: Difference and Dominance*. Rowley, Mass.: Newbury House.

Bogoras, W. (1922). Chukchee. In F. Boas (ed.), *Handbook of American Indian Languages*, BAE–B40 (Part 2). Washington, DC: Smithsonian Institute.

Borker, R. A. (1980). Anthropology: social and cultural perspectives. In S. McConnell-Ginet, R. Barker and N. Firman (eds), *Women and Language in Literature and Society*. New York: Praeger.

Bornstein, M. H. (1975). The influence of visual perception on culture. *American Anthropologist, 77,* 774–98.

Bradley, P. H. (1980). Sex, competence and opinion deviation: An expectation states approach. *Communication Monographs, 47,* 101–10.

Bradley, P. H. (1981). The folk-linguistics of women's speech: An empirical examination. *Communication Monographs, 48,* 73–90.

Brazil, D. (1978). *Discourse and Intonation II*. Birmingham: University of Birmingham, English Language Research.

Brend, R. M. (1975). Male–female interaction patterns in American English. In B. Thorne and N. Henley (eds), *Language and Sex: Difference and Dominance*. Rowley, Mass: Newbury House.

Brooks, L. (1974). Interactive effects of sex and status on self-disclosure. *Journal of Counseling Psychology, 21,* 469–74.

Brotherton, P. L. and Penman, R. A. (1977). A comparison of some characteristics of male and female speech. *Journal of Social Psychology, 103,* 161–2.

Brouwer, D. (1982). The influence of the addressee's sex on politeness in language use. *Linguistics, 20,* 697–711.

Brouwer, D., Gerritsen, M. and De Haan, D. (1979). Speech differences between women and men: on the wrong track? *Language and Society, 8,* 33-50.

Broverman, I. K., Broverman, D M., Clarkson, F. E., Rosenkrantz, P, S and Vogel, S. R. (1970). Sex role stereotypes and clinical judgements of mental health. *Journal of Consulting and Clinical Psychology, 34,* 1–7.

Broverman, I. K., Vogel, S. R., Broverman, D. M., Clarkson, F. E. and Rosenkrantz, P. S. (1972). Sex role stereotypes. A current appraisal. *Journal of Social Issues, 28,* 59–78.

Brown, J. D. (1981). Adolescent peer group communication, sex-role norms and decisions about occupations. *Communication Yearbook,* vol. 4. New Brunswick, NJ: Transaction.

Brown, P. (1980). How and why are women more polite: some evidence from a Mayan community. In S. McConnell-Ginet, R. Borker and N. Furman (eds), *Women and Language in Literature and Society.* New York: Praeger.

Brown, R. (1965). *Social Psychology.* London: Collier Macmillan.

Cappell, A. (1966). *Studies in Socio-linguistics.* The Hague: Mouton.

Carson, R. C. (1969). *Interaction Concepts of Personality.* Chicago: Aldine.

Chambers, J. K. and Trudgill, P. (1980). *Dialectology.* Cambridge: Cambridge University Press.

Chelune, G. J. (1979). Measuring openness in interpersonal communication. In G. J. Chelune *et al.* (eds), *Self-disclosure: Origins, Patterns and Implications in Interpersonal Relations.* San Francisco: Jossey-Bass.

Cherry, L. and Lewis, M. (1975). *Mothers and Two-Year-Olds: A Study of Sex-Differentiated Aspects of Verbal Interaction.* Princeton, NJ: Educational Testing Service Research Bulletin.

Cheshire, J. (1978). Present verbs in reading English. In P. Trudgill (ed.), *Sociolinguistic Patterns in British English.* London: Edward Arnold, 52–68.

Cheyne, W. M. (1970). Stereotyped reactions to speakers with Scottish and English regional accents. *British Journal of Clinical and Social Psychology, 9,* 77–9.

Cicone, M. V. and Ruble, D. N. (1978). Beliefs about males. *Journal of Social Issues, 34* (1), 5–16.

Coleman, R. O. (1971). Male and female voice quality and its relationship to vowel formant frequencies. *Journal of Speech and Hearing Research, 14* (3), 565–77.

Coleman, R. O. (1976). A comparison of the contributions of two voice quality characteristics to the perception of maleness and femaleness in the voice. *Journal of Speech and Hearing Research, 19,* 168-80.

Condry, J. and Condry, S. (1976). Sex differences: A study in the eye of the beholder. *Child Development, 47,* 812–19.

Constantinople, A. (1973). Masculinity–femininity: An exception to a famous dictum? *Psychological Bulletin, 80,* (5), 389–407.

Courtney, A. E. and Whipple, T. W. (1974). Women in TV commercials. *Journal of Communication, 24,* 110–17.

Coussins, J. (1976). *The Equality Report.* London: National Council for Civil Liberties.

Crosby, F. and Nyquist, L. (1977). The female register: An empirical study of Lakoff's hypotheses. *Language in Society, 6,* 313–22.

Crosby, F., Jose, P. and Wong-McCarthy, W. (1981). Gender, androgyny and conversational assertiveness. In C. Mayo and N. Henley (eds), *Gender and Non-verbal Communication.* New York: Springer-Verlag.

Crouch, I. and Dubois, B. L. (1977). Interpersonal communication in the classroom: Whose speech is inferior? Unpublished manuscript, New Mexico State University.

Crystal, D. (1971). Prosodic and paralinguistic correlates of social categories. In E. Ardener (ed), *Social Anthropology and Language.* London: Tavistock Press.

Crystal, D. (1975). *The English Tone of Voice.* London: Edward Arnold.

Dahlstrom, W. G. and Welsh, G. S. (1960). *An MMPI Handbook.* Minneapolis: University of Minnesota Press.

Davis, J. D. (1978). When boy meets girl: Sex roles and the negotiation of intimacy in an acquaintance exercise. *Journal of Personality and Social Psychology, 36* (7), 684–92.

Deaux, K. (1984). From individual differences to social categories: analysis of a decade's research on gender. *American Psychologist, 39* (2), 105–16.

Deaux, K. and Emswiller, T. (1974). Explanations for successful performance on sex-linked tasks: What is skill for the male is luck for the female. *Journal of Personality and Social Psychology, 29,* 80–85.

Derlega, V. J. and Grzelak, A. L. (1979). Appropriateness of self-disclosure. In G. J. Chelune (ed.), *Self-disclosure: Origins, Patterns, and Implications of Openness in Interpersonal Relationships.* San Francisco, Jossey-Bass.

DeVogue, J. T. and Beck, S. (1978). The therapist–client relationship in behavior therapy. In M. Herson, R. M. Eisler and P. M. Miller (eds), *Progress in Behavior Modification*, vol. 6. New York: Academic Press.

Doise, W. (1978). *Groups and Individuals: Explanations in Social Psychology*. Cambridge: Cambridge University Press.

Dubois, B. L. and Crouch I. (1975) The question of tag questions in women's speech: They don't really use more of them, do they? *Language in Society*, 4, 289–94.

Duncan, S. and Fiske, D. (1977). *Face-to-face Interaction: Research, Methods and Theory*. Hillsdale, NJ: Lawrence Erlbaum Associates.

Eakins, B. and Eakins, G. (1976). Verbal turn-taking and exchanges in faculty dialogue. In B. L. Dubois and I. Crouch (eds), *The Sociology of the Lunguages of American Women*. San Antonio, Texas: Trinity University Press.

Eakins, B. and Eakins, G. (1978). *Sex Differences in Human Communication*. Boston: Houghton Mifflin.

Edelsky, C. (1976a). The acquisition of communicative competence. Recognition of linguistic correlates of sex roles. *Merrill-Palmer Quarterly*, 22 (1), 47–59.

Edelsky, C. (1976b). Subjective reactions to sex-linked language. *Journal of Social Psychology*, 99, 97–104.

Edwards, J. R. (1979). Social class and the identification of sex in children's speech. *Child Language*, 6, 121–7.

Ekka, F. (1972). Men's and women's speech in Kurux. *Linguistics*, 81, 25–31.

Elyan, O. (1978). Sex differences in speech style. *Women Speaking*, 4, 4–8.

Elyan, O., Smith, P. M., Giles, H. and Bourhis, R. (1978). RP accented female speech: The voice of perceived androgyny? In P. Trudgill (ed.), *Sociolinguistic Patterns in British English*. London: Edward Arnold, 122–31.

Equal Opportunities Commission (1979). *Research Bulletin*, 1 (2).

Erickson, B., Lind, E. A., Johnson, B. C. and O'Barr, W. M. (1978). Speech style and impression formation in a court setting: The effects of 'Powerful' and 'Powerless' speech. *Journal of Experimental Social Psychology*, 14, 266–79.

Falbo, T. (1977). Multidimensional scaling of power strategies. *Journal of Personality and Social Psychology*, 35, 537–47.

Fasold, R. W. (1968). *A Sociolinguistic Study of the Pronunciation of Three Vowels in Detroit Speech*. Washington, DC: Center for Applied Linguistics.

Fasold, R. W. (1972). *Tense Marking in Black English: A Linguistic and Social Analysis*. Washington DC: Center for Applied Linguistics.

Feather, N. T. and Simon, J. G. (1973). Fear of success and causal attributions for outcome. *Journal of Personality, 41,* 525–42.

Feirstein, B. (1982). *Real Men Don't Eat Quiche: A Guidebook to All that is Truly Masculine.* New York: Pocket Books.

Fischer, J. L. (1958). Social influences on the choice of a linguistic variant. *Word, 14,* 47–56.

Fishman, P. (1978). Interaction: The work women do. *Social Problems, 25,* 397–406.

Fishman, P. (1980). Conversational insecurity. In H. Giles, W. P. Robinson and P. M. Smith, (eds), *Language: Social Psychological Perspectives.* Oxford: Pergamon Press, 127–32.

Foa, U. G. (1961). Convergences in the analysis of the structure of interpersonal behaviour. *Psychological Review, 68,* 341–58.

Forgas, J. P. (1979). *Social Episodes: The Study of Interaction Routines.* New York and London: Academic Press.

Friend, P., Kalin, R. and Giles, H. (1979). Sex bias in the evaluation of journal articles: Sexism in England. *British Journal of Social and Clinical Psychology, 18,* 77–8.

Frost, J. H. (1977). The influence of female and male communication styles on conflict strategies: Problem areas. Paper presented at the International Communication Association Convention, Berlin, West Germany.

Fuller, F. (1960). Influence of sex of counselor and client on client expressions of feeling during counselling. Unpublished PhD dissertation, Department of Psychology, University of Texas at Austin.

Gardner, R. C. (1973). Ethnic stereotypes: The traditional approach, a new look. *Canadian Psychologist, 14,* 133–48.

Garry, L. (ed.) (1973). *The Standard Periodical Directory,* 4th edn. New York: Oxbridge.

Gershuny, H. L. (1977). Sexism in the language of literature. In A. P. Nilsen, H. Bosmajian, H. L. Gershuny and J. P. Stanley (eds), *Sexism and Language.* Urbana, Illinois: National Council of Teachers of English.

Giles, H. (1978). Linguistic differentiation in ethnic groups. In H. Tajfel (ed.), *Differentiation Between Social Groups.* London: Academic Press.

Giles, H. (1979). Ethnicity markers in speech. In K. Scherer and H. Giles (eds), *Social Markers in Speech.* Cambridge: Cambridge University Press.

Giles, H. and Marsh, P. (1979). Perceived masculinity and accented speech. *Language Sciences, 1,* 301–15.

Giles, H. and Powesland, P. (1975). *Speech Style and Social Evaluation*. London: Academic Press.

Giles, H., Smith, P., Ford, B., Condor, S. and Thakerar, J. (1980). Speech style and the fluctuating saliency of sex. *Language Sciences, 2* (2), 260–82.

Goffman, E. (1976). Gender advertisements. *Studies in the Anthropology of Visual Communication, 3,* 65–154.

Goffman, E. (1977). The arrangement between the sexes. *Theory and Society, 4,* 301–31.

Gough, H. G. (1966). A cross-cultural analysis of the CPI Femininity Scale. *Journal of Consulting Psychology, 30,* 136–41.

Graham, A. (1975). The making of a nonsexist dictionary. In D. Thorne and N. Henley (eds), *Language and Sex: Difference and Dominance.* Rowley, Mass.: Newbury House.

Graham, J. A., Argyle, M. and Furnham, A. (1980). The goal structure of situations. *European Journal of Social Psychology, 10,* 345–66.

Guidelines for Equal Treatment of the Sexes (1972). New York: McGraw-Hill.

Guidelines for Improving the Image of Women in Textbooks (1972). Glenview, Ill.: Scott, Foresman & Co.

Guilford, J. P. and Guilford, R. B. (1936). Personality factors S, E and M and their measurement. *Journal of Psychology, 2,* 109–27.

Gumperz, J. J. (1982). *Discourse Strategies.* Cambridge: Cambridge University Press.

Gutzman, H. R. Sr and Flatau, T. S. (1906). Die Stimme des Sauglings. *Archives of Laryngology, 18* (2).

Haas, A. (1979). Male and female spoken language differences: Stereotypes and evidence. *Psychological Bulletin, 86* (3), 616–26.

Haas, M. R. (1944). Men's and women's speech in Koasati. *Language, 20,* 142–9.

Hakim, C. (1979). *Occupational Segregation: A Comparative Study of the Degree and Pattern of the Differentiation Between Men and Women's Work in Britain, the United States and Other Countries. Research Paper No. 9.* London: HMSO/Department of Employment.

Harris, M. B. (1977). The effects of gender, masculinity–femininity and trait favorability on evaluations of students. *Contemporary Educational Psychology, 2,* 353–63.

Harrison, L. (1975). Cro-Magnan women – in eclipse. *The Science Teacher, 42,* (4), 8–11.

Hartmann, M. (1976). A descriptive study of the language of men and women born in Maine around 1900. In B. L. Dubois and I. Crouch (eds), *Papers in Southwest English IV: Proceedings of the Conference on the Sociology of the Languages of American Women.* San Antonio, Texas: Trinity University Press.

Head, B. (1977). Sex as a factor in the use of obscenity. Paper presented at the Linguistic Society of America Summer Meeting, Honolulu.

Heilbrun, A. B. (1973). Parent identification and filial sex-role behavior: The importance of biological context. In J. K. Cole and R. Dienstbier (eds), *Nebraska Symposium on Motivation,* vol. 21. Lincoln: University of Nebraska Press.

Heilbrun, A. B. (1976). Measurement of masculine and feminine sex role identities as independent dimensions. *Journal of Consulting and Clinical Psychology, 44,* 183–90.

Heilbrun, A. B. (1981). Gender differences in the functional linkage between androgyny, social cognition and competence. *Journal of Personality and Social Psychology, 41,* (6), 1106–18.

Hill, C. E. (1975). Sex of client and sex and experience level of counselor. *Journal of Counseling Psychology, 22,* 6–11.

Hilpert, F. P., Kramer, C. and Clark, R. A. (1975). Participant's perceptions of self and partner in mixed-sex dyads. *Central States Speech Journal, 26,* 52–6.

Hirschman, L. (1973). Analysis of supportive and assertive behavior in conversation. Paper presented at the Linguistic Society of America Summer Meeting, Amherst.

Hirschman, L. (1974). Female–male differences in conversational interaction. Paper presented at the meeting of the Linguistic Society of America, December 1973. Cited in B. Thorne and N. Henley (eds), *Language of Sex: Difference and Dominance.* Rowley, Mass.: Newbury House.

Hollien, H. and Shipp, T. (1972). Speaking fundamental frequency and chronologic age in males. *Journal of Speech and Hearing Research, 15,* 155–9.

Howitt, D. (1982). *The Mass Media and Social Problems.* Oxford: Pergamon Press.

Hudson, R. A. (1980). *Sociolinguistics.* Cambridge: Cambridge University Press.

Hudson, R. A. and Holloway, A. F. (1977). Variation in London English. Unpublished report to the Social Science Research Council of Great Britain on Grant 4595.

Hutt, C. (1972). *Males and Females.* Harmondsworth, Middlesex: Penguin Books.

Ickes, W. and Barnes, R. D. (1978). Boys and girls together – and alienated: On enacting stereotyped sex roles in mixed-sex dyads. *Journal of Personality and Social Psychology, 36,* 669–83.

Ingeman, F. (1968). Identification of the speaker's sex from voiceless fricatives. *Journal of the Acoustical Society of America, 44,* 1142–4.

International Labour Office (1976). *Women Workers and Society: International Perspectives.* Geneva: International Labour Office.

Jenkin, N. and Vroegh, K. (1969). Contemporary concepts of masculinity and femininity. *Psychological Reports, 25,* 679–97.

Jespersen, O. (1922). *Language: Its Nature, Development and Origin.* London: Allen and Unwin.

Jorden, E. (1974). Language – female and feminine. In B. Hoffer (ed.), *Proceedings of a US-Japanese Sociolinguistics Meeting.* San Antonio, Texas: Trinity University Press.

Jose, P. E., Crosby, F. and Wong-McCarthy, W. J. (1980) Androgyny, dyadic compatibility and conversational behaviour. Unpublished manuscript, Yale University.

Jourard, S. M.. (1971). *Self-disclosure: An Experimental Analysis of the Transparent Self.* New York: John Wiley.

Kelly, J. A. and Worell, J. (1977). New formulations of sex roles and androgyny: A critical review. *Journal of Consulting and Clinical Psychology, 45* (6), 1101-15.

Kessler, S. J. and McKenna, W. (1978). *Gender: An Ethnomethodological Approach.* New York: John Wiley.

Key, M. R. (1972). Linguistic behaviour of male and female. *Linguistics, 88,* 15–31.

Key, M. R. (1975). *Male/Female Language.* Metuchen, NJ: Scarecrow Press.

Kiesler, D. J. (1983). The 1982 interpersonal circle: A taxonomy for complementarity in human transactions. *Psychological Review, 90* (3), 185–214.

Kramarae, C. (1981). *Women and Men Speaking: Frameworks for Analysis.* Rowley, Mass.: Newbury House.

Kramer, C. (1974). Stereotypes of women's speech: The word from cartoons. *Journal of Popular Culture, 8,* 624–30.

Kramer, C. (1975). Sex-linked differences in address systems. *Anthropological Linguistics, 17,* 198–210.

Kramer, C. (1978). Male and female perceptions of male and female speech. *Language and Speech, 20* (2), 151–61.

Labov, W. (1963). The social motivation of a sound change. *Word, 19,* 273–309.

Labov, W. (1966). *The Social Stratification of English in New York City.* Washington, DC: Center for Applied Linguistics.

Labov, W. (1970). The study of language in its social context. *Studium Generale, 23, 30–87.*

Labov, W. (1972). *Sociolinguistic Patterns*. Philadelphia: University of Pennsylvania Press.

Ladd, D. R. (1978). *The Structure of Intonational Meaning*. Unpublished PhD dissertation, Cornell University, Ithaca, New York.

Lakoff, R. (1973). Language and woman's place. *Language in Society, 2*, 45–80.

Lakoff, R. (1975). *Language and Woman's Place*. New York: Harper and Row.

Lakoff, R. (1977). Women's language. *Language and Style, 10* (4), 222–47.

Lambert, W. (1967). A social psychology of bilingualism. *Journal of Social Issues, 23*, 91–109.

Land, H. (1978). Sex role stereotyping in the social security and income tax systems. In J. Chetwynd and O. Hartnett (eds), *The Sex Role System*. London: Routledge and Kegan Paul.

Landis, C. (1927). National differences in conversation. *Journal of Abnormal and Social Psychology, 21*, 354–75.

Landis, M. H. and Burtt, H. E. (1924). A study of conversation. *Journal of Comparative Psychology, 4*, 81–9.

Lanham, L. W. and Macdonald, C. A. (1977). *The Standard in South African English and its Social History*. Unpublished manuscript, University of Witwatersrand, Johannesburg.

Lass, N. J ., Hughes, K. R., Bowyer, M. D., Waters, L. T. and Bourne, V. T. (1976). Speaker sex identification from voiced, whispered and filtered isolated vowels. *Journal of Acoustical Society of America, 59*, 675–8.

Lass, N. J., Mertz, P. J. and Kimmel, K. L. (1978). The effect of temporal speech alterations on speaker race and sex identifications. *Language and Speech, 21* (3), 279–91.

Lazer, C. and Dier, S. (1978). The labor force in fiction. *Journal of Communication, 28*, 174–82.

Leary, T. (1957). *Interpersonal Diagnosis of Personality*. New York: Ronald Press.

Leet-Pellegrini, H. M. (1980). Conversational dominance as function of gender and expertise. PhD dissertation, Tufts University.

Levine, L. and Crockett, H. R. Jr (1966). Speech variation in a Piedmont community: Postvocalic r. In S. Lieberson (ed.), *Explorations in Sociolinguistics*. The Hague: Mouton.

Lieberman, P. (1967). *Intonation, Perception and Language*. Cambridge: Cambridge University Press.

Lippa, R., Valdez, E. and Jolly, A. (1983). The effects of self-monitoring on the expressive display of masculinity–femininity. *Journal of Research in Personality, 17,* 324–38.

Luchsinger, R. and Arnold, G. F. (1965). Development and involution of the voice. In R. Luchsinger and G. F. Arnold (eds), *Voice-Speech-Language; Clinical Communicology: Its Physiology and Pathology.* Belmont CA: Wadsworth Press.

Lunneborg, P. (1972). Dimensionality of MF. *Journal of Clinical Psychology, 28,* 313–17.

Lunneborg, P. and Lunneborg, C. W. (1970). Factor structure of MF scales and items. *Journals of Clinical Psychology, 26,* 360–6.

Macaulay, R. K. S. (1978). Variation and consistency in Glaswegian English. In P. Trudgill (ed.), *Sociolinguistic Patterns in British English.* London: Edward Arnold.

MacCormack, C. P. and Strathern, M. (eds) (1980). *Nature, Culture and Gender.* Cambridge: Cambridge University Press.

Mackay, D. G. (1980). Psychology, prescriptive grammar, and the pronoun problem. *American Psychologist, 35* (5), 444–9.

MacKay, D. G. and Fulkerson, D. (1979). On the comprehension and production of pronouns. *Journal of Verbal Learning and Verbal Behaviour, 18,* 661–73.

Maltz, D. N. and Borker, R. A. (1982). A cultural approach to male–female communication. In J. J. Gumperz (ed.), *Language and Social Identity.* Cambridge: Cambridge University Press.

Maracek, J., Piliavin, J. A., Fitzsimmons, E., Krogh, E. C., Leader, E. and Trudgill, B. J(1978). Women as TV experts: The voice of authority? *Journal of Communication, 28,* 159–68.

Markel, N. N., Long, J. F. and Saine, T. J. (1976). Sex effects in conversational interaction: Another look at male dominance. *Human Communication Research, 2,* 356–64.

Martin, M. K. and Voorhies, B. (1975). *Female of the Species.* New York: Columbia University Press.

Martyna, W. (1980). The psychology of generic masculine. In S. McConnell-Ginet, R. Borker and N. Furman (eds), *Women and Languge in Literature and Society,* 69–78. New York: Praeger.

Mattingly, I. G. (1966). Speaker variation and vocal tract size. *Journal of the Acoustical Society of America, 39,* 1219.

McConnell-Ginet, S. (1978a). Intonation in a man's world. *Signs: Journal of Women in Culture and Society, 3* (3), 541–59.

McConnell-Ginet, S. (1978b). Intonation in the social context: Language and sex. Paper presented at the Ninth International Congress in Sociology, Uppsala, Sweden.

McConnell-Ginet, S. (1979). Prototypes, pronouns and persons. In

M. Mathiot (ed.), *Ethnolinguistics: Boas, Sapir and Whorf Revisited.* The Hague: Mouton.

McConnell-Ginet, S., Borker, R. and Furman, N. (1980). *Women and Language in Literature and Society.* New York: Praeger.

McGlone, J., Hollien, H. and Moore, P. (1965). Speaking fundamental frequency characteristics of 15, 16 and 17-year-old girls. *Language and Speech, 9,* 46.

McGlone, R. and Hollien, H. (1963). Vocal pitch characteristics of aged women. *Journal of Speech and Hearing Research, 6,* 164.

Miller, C. and Swift, K. (1976). *Words and Women: New Language in New Times.* Garden City, NY: Doubleday Anchor.

Miller, M. D. (1982). Friendship, power and the language of compliance-gaining. *Journal of Language and Social Psychology, 1* (2), 111–22.

Milner, D. (1981). Racial prejudice. In J. C. Turner and H. Giles (eds), *Intergroup Behaviour.* Oxford: Basil Blackwell.

Milroy, L. (1980). *Language and Social Networks.* Oxford: Basil Blackwell.

Money, J. and Ehrhardt, A. A. (1972). *Man and Woman, Boy and Girl.* Baltimore: Johns Hopkins University Press.

Moore, H. T. (1922). Further data concerning sex differences. *Journal of Abnormal and Social Psychology, 4,* 81–9.

Morton, T. L. (1978). Intimacy and reciprocity of exchange: A comparison of spouses and strangers. *Journal of Personality and Social Psychology, 36,* 72–81.

Murray, T., Amundson, P. and Hollien, H. (1977). Acoustical characteristics of infant cries: Fundamental frequency. *Journal of Child Language, 4,* 321–8.

Murray, T., Hollien, H. and Muller, E. (1975). Perceptual responses to infant crying: Identification of cry types. *Journal of Child Language, 1,* 89–95.

Myers, A. M. and Gonda, G. (1982a). Empirical validation of the Bem Sex Role Inventory. *Journal of Personality and Social Psychology, 43* (2), 304–18.

Myers, A. M. and Gonda, G. (1982b). Utility of the masculinity femininity construct: Comparison of traditional and androgyny approaches. *Journal of Personality and Social Psychology, 43* (3), 514–22.

Nichols, R. C. (1962). Subtle, obvious and stereotype measures of masculinity–femininity. *Educational and Psychological Measurement, 22,* 449–61.

Nilsen, A. P. (1977a). Linguistic sexism as a social issue. In A. P.

Nilsen, H. Bosmajian, J. L. Gershuny and J. P. Stanley (eds), *Sexism and Language*. Urbana, Illinois: National Council of Teachers of English, 1–26.

Nilsen, A. P. (1977b). Sexism as shown through the English vocabulary. In A. P. Nilsen, H. Bosmajian, H. L. Gershuny and J. P. Stanley (eds), *Sexism and Language*. Urbana, Illinois: National Council of Teachers of English, 27–42.

Nilsen, A. P. (1977c). Sexism in the language of marriage. In A. P. Nilsen *et al.*, *Sexism and Language*. Urbana, Illinois: National Council of Teachers of English.

Nilsen, A. P. Bosmajian, H., Gershuny, J. L. and Stanley, J. P. (1977). *Sexism and Language*. Urbana, Illinois: National Council of Teachers of English.

O'Barr, W. M. and Atkins, B. K. (1980). 'Women's language' or 'powerless language'. In S. McConnell-Ginet, R. Borker and N. Furman (eds), *Women and Language in Literature and Society*. New York: Praeger, 93–110.

Oftedal, M. (1973). Notes on language and sex. *Norwegian Journal of Linguistics (NTS), 27,* 67–75.

Osgood, C. E., Suci, G. J. and Tannenbaum, P. H. (1957). *The Measurement of Meaning*. Urbana, Ill.: University of Illinois Press

Parsons, J. E., Frieze, I. J. and Ruble, C. N. (1976). Introduction. *Journal of Social Issues, 32* (3), 1–5.

Parson, T. and Bales, R. F. (1955). *Family Socialization and Interaction Process*. Glencoe, Ill.: Free Press.

Patton, B. R., Jasnoski, M. and Sherchock, L. (1977). Communication implications of androgyny. Paper presented at the annual convention of the Speech Communication Association, Washington, DC.

Pedersen, T. B. (1980). Sex and communication: A brief presentation of an experimental approach. In H. Giles, W. P. Robinson and P. M. Smith (eds), *Language: Social Psychological Perspectives*. Oxford: Pergamon Press, 105–14.

Pedhazur, E. J. and Tetenbaum, T. J. (1979). Bem Sex Role Inventory: A theoretical and methodological critique. *Journal of Personality and Social Psychology, 37* (6), 996–1016.

Pellowe, J. and Jones, V. (1978). On intonational variability in Tyneside speech. In P. Trudgill (ed.), *Sociolinguistic Patterns in British English*. London: Edward Arnold, 101–21.

Peterson, G. E. and Barney, H. L. (1952). Control methods used in a study of the vowels. *Journal of the Acoustical Society of America, 24,* 175–84.

Petty, R. E. and Caccioppo, J. T. (1981). *Attitudes and Persuasion:*

Classic and Contemporary Approaches. Dubuque, Iowa: Wm C. Brown.

Putnam, L. and McAllister, L. (1981). Situational effects of task and gender on nonverbal display. *Communication Yearbook,* vol. 4. New Brunswick, NJ: Transaction.

Reid, I. and Wormald, E. (1982). *Sex Differences in Britain*. London: Grant McIntyre.

Roger, D. B. and Schumacher, A. (1984). The effects of individual differences on dyadic conversation strategies. *Journal of Personality and Social Psychology, 45* (3), 700–5.

Romaine, S. (1982). *Socio-historical Linguistics: Its Status and Methodology*. Cambridge: Cambridge University Press.

Romaine, S. and Reid, E. (1976). Glottal sloppiness? A sociolinguistic view of urban speech in Scotland. *Teaching English, 9* (3), 12–16.

Rosch, E. (1977). Human categorization. In N. Warren (ed.), *Advances in Cross-cultural Psychology,* vol. 1. London: Academic Press.

Rosenkrantz, P. L., Vogel, S. R., Bee, H., Broverman, I. K. and Broverman, D. M. (1968). Sex-role stereotypes and self-concepts in college students. *Journal of Consulting and Clinical Psychology, 32,* 287–95.

Rowbotham, S. (1973). *Hidden form History*. London: Pluto Press.

Rubin, J. Z., Provenzano, F. J. and Luria, Z. (1974). The eye of the beholder: Parents' views on sex of newborns. *American Journal of Orthopsychiatry, 44* (4), 512–19.

Ruble, D. N. and Higgins, E. T. (1976). Effects of group sex and composition on self-presentation and sex-typing. *Journal of Social Issues, 32* (3), 125–32.

Ryan, P. M. (1981). An introduction to Hausa personal nomenclature. *Names, 29,* 139–64.

Sachs, A. and Wilson, J. H. (1978). *Sexism and the Law*. London: Martin Robinson.

Sachs, J. (1975). Cues to the identification of sex in children's speech. In B. Thorne and N. Henley (eds), *Sex and Language: Difference and Dominance*. Rowley, Mass.: Newbury House.

Sachs, J., Lieberman, P and Erickson, D. (1973). Anatomical and cultural determinants of male and female speech. In R. W. Shuy and R. W. Fasold (eds), *Language Attitudes: Current Trends and Prospects*. Washington, DC: Georgetown University Press, 74–84.

Sankoff, G. and Cedergren, H. (1971). Some results of a sociolinguistic study of Montreal French. In R. Darnell (ed.), *Linguistic Diversity in Canadian Society*. Edmonton and Champaign: Linguistic Research Inc.

Schneider, J. W. and Hacker, S. L. (1973). Sex role imagery and use of the generic 'man' in introductory texts: A case in the sociology of sociology. *American Sociologist, 8,* 12–18.

Schulz, M. (1975). The semantic derogation of woman. In B. Thorne and N. Henley (eds), *Language and Sex: Difference and Dominance.* Rowley, Mass.: Newbury House.

Schwartz, M. F. (1968). Identification of speaker sex from isolated voiceless fricatives. *Journal of Acoustical Society of America, 43,* 1178–9.

Schwartz, M. F. and Rine, H. E. (1968) Identification of speaker sex from isolated, whispered vowels. *Journal of Acoustical Society of America, 44,* 1736–7.

Seavey, C. A., Katz, P. A. and Zalk, S. R. (1975). The effect of gender labels on adult responses to infants. *Sex Roles, 1* (2), 103–9.

Shaw, M. and Costanzo, P. R. (1982). *Theories of Social Psychology.* New York: McGraw-Hill.

Sherman, J. A. (1976). Social values, femininity, and the development of female competence. *Journals of Social Issues, 32* (3), 181–96.

Shuy, R. W., Wolfram, W. A. and Riley, W. K. (1967). *Linguistic Correlates of Social Stratification in Detroit Speech.* Washington, DC: US Office of Education.

Siegler, D. M. and Siegler, R. S. (1976). Stereotypes of males' and females' speech. *Psychological Reports, 39,* 167–70.

Smith, P. M. (1979). Sex markers in speech. In K. Scherer and H. Giles (eds), *Social Markers in Speech.* Cambridge: Cambridge University Press, 109–46.

Smith, P. M. (1981). Language variables in intergroup relations: The voices of masculinity and femininity. Unpublished PhD dissertation, Bristol University.

Smith, P. M., Giles, H. and Hewstone, M. (1980). Sociolinguistics: A social psychological perspective. In R. N. St Clair and H. Giles (eds), *The Social and Psychological Contexts of Language.* Hillsdale, NJ: Lawrence Erlbaum Associates, 283–98.

Smith, P. M., Giles, H. and Hewstone, M. (1983). New horizons in the study of speech and social situations. In B. Bain (ed.), *The Sociogenesis of Language and Human Conduct.* New York and London: Plenum Press.

Soskin, W. F. and John, V. P. (1963). The study of spontaneous talk. In R. Barker (ed.), *The Stream of Behavior.* New York: Appleton-Century-Crofts.

Spence, J. T. and Helmreich, R. L. (1978). *Masculinity and Femininity: Their Psychological Dimensions, Correlates, and Antecedents.*

Austin, Texas: University of Texas Press.

Spence, J. T. and Helmreich, R. L. (1980). The many faces of androgyny: A reply to Locksley and Colten. *Journal of Personality and Social Psychology, 37* (6), 1032–46.

Spence, J. T., Helmreich, R. L. and Stapp, J. (1975). Ratings of self and peers on sex role attributes and their relation to self-esteem and conceptions of masculinity and femininity. *Journal of Personality and Social Psychology, 32,* 29–39.

Spender, D. (1980). *Man Made Language.* London, Boston, and Henley: Routledge and Kegan Paul.

Spender, D. (1983). *Women of Ideas: And What Men Have Done to Them: From Aphra Behn to Adrienne Rich.* London: Routledge and Kegan Paul.

Stake, J. E. and Stake, M. N. (1976). Performance self-esteem and dominance behavior in mixed-sex dyads.

Stanley, J. P. (1977a). Paradigmatic women: The prostitute. In D. L. Shores and C. P. Hines (eds), *Papers in Language Variation.* University of Alabama: University of Alabama Press.

Stanley, J. P. (1977b). Gender marking in American English: Usage and reference. In A. P. Nilsen *et al., Sexism and Language.* Urbana, Illinois: National Council of Teachers of English.

Stannard, U. (1977). *Mrs Man.* San Francisco: Germainbooks.

Stoppard, J. M. (1976). Personality characteristics in gender stereotypes and sex roles. Unpublished PhD dissertation, Queens University, Canada.

Stoppard, J. M. and Kalin, R. (1978). Can gender stereotypes and sex-role conceptions be distinguished? *British Journal of Social and Clinical Psychology, 17,* 211–17.

Strahan, F. (1975). Remarks on Bem's measurement of psychological androgyny: Alternatives, methods and a supplementary analysis. *Journal of Consulting and Clinical Psychology, 43,* 568–71.

Strathern, M. (1976). An anthropological perspective. In B. Lloyd and J. Archer (eds), *Exploring Sex Differences.* London: Academic Press, 49–70.

Strodbeck, F. L. (1951). Husband–wife interaction over revealed differences. *American Sociological Review, 16,* 468–73.

Strong, E. K. (1943). *Vocational Interests of Men and Women.* Stanford, California: Stanford University Press.

Sullivan, H. S. (1953). *The Interpersonal Theory of Psychiatry.* New York: W. W. Norton.

Swacker, M. (1975). The sex of the speaker as a sociolinguistic variable.

In B. Thorne and N. Henley (eds), *Language and Sex: Difference and Dominance.*

Tajfel, H. (1978a). The psychological structure of intergroup relations. In H. Tajfel (ed.), *Differentiation Between Social Groups: Studies in the Social Psychology of Intergroup Relations.* London: Academic Press, 27–98.

Tajfel, H. (1978b). *The Social Psychology of Minorities.* London: Minority Rights Group.

Tajfel, H. (1981). Social stereotypes and social groups. In J. C. Turner and H. Giles (eds), *Intergroup Behaviour.* Oxford: Basil Blackwell, 144–67.

Tajfel, H. (ed.) (1982). *Social Identity and Intergroup Relations.* Cambridge: Cambridge University Press.

Tajfel, H. and Turner, J. C. (1979). Towards an integrative theory of intergroup conflict. In W. G. Austin and S. Worchel (eds), *The Social Psychology of Intergroup Relations.* Monterey, California: Brooks/Cole, 33–48.

Takefuta, Y., Jancosek, E. G. and Brunt, M. (1971). A statistical analysis of melody curves in the intonation of American English. *Proceedings of the 7th Congress of Phonetic Sciences.* The Hague: Mouton.

Tanner, J. M. (1978). *Foetus Into Man.* London: Open Books.

Tavard, G. H. (1977). Sexist language in theology? In W. Burkhardt (ed.), *Woman: New Dimensions.* New York: Paulist Press.

Taylor, D. (1951). Sex gender in Central American Carib. *International Journal of American Linguistics, 17* (2), 102–4.

Taylor, D. M. (1981). Stereotypes and intergroup relations. In R. C. Gardener and R. Kalin (eds), *A Canadian Social Psychology of Ethnic Relations.* Toronto: Methuen. 151–71.

Taylor, M. C. and Hall, J. A. (1982). Psychological androgyny: Theories, methods and conclusions. *Psychological Bulletin, 92* (2), 347–66.

Terman, L. and Miles, C. C. (1936). *Sex and Personality.* New York: McGraw-Hill.

Terrango, L. (1966). Pitch and duration characteristics on the oral reading of males on a masculinity–femininity dimension. *Journal of Speech and Hearing Research, 9,* 590–5.

Thorne, B. and Henley, N. (1975). Difference and dominance: An overview of language, gender and society. In B. Thorne and N. Henley (eds), *Language and Sex: Difference and Dominance.* Rowley, Mass.: Newbury House, 5–42.

Tilby, P. J. and Kalin, R. (1977). Effect of sex-role deviant life-styles in otherwise normal persons on the perception of maladjustment. Unpublished manuscript, Queens University, Canada.

Treichler, P. A. (1984). Women, Language and Health Care: An Annotated bibliography. *Women and Language News, 7* (2/3), 7–19.

Treichler, P. A. and Kramarae, C. (1983). Women's talk in the ivory tower. *Communication Quarterly, 31* (2), 118–32.

Trudgill, P. (1975). Sex, covert prestige and linguistic change in the urban British English of Norwich. In B. Thorne and N. Henley (eds), *Sex and Language: Difference and Dominance*. Rowley, Mass.: Newbury House.

Trudgill, P. (ed.) (1978). *Sociolinguistic Patterns in British English*. London: Edward Arnold.

Trudgill, P. (1983). *Sociolinguistics: An Introduction to Language and Society*. Harmondsworth: Penguin.

Turner, J. C. (1981). The experimental social psychology of intergroup behaviour. In J. C. and H. Giles (eds) *Intergroup Behaviour*. Oxford: Basil Blackwell.

Turner, J. C. (1982). Towards a cognitive redefinition of the social group. In H. Tajfel (ed.), *Social Identity and Intergroup Relations*. Cambridge: Cambridge University Press, 15–40.

Turner, J. C. and Brown, R. J. (1978). Social status, cognitive alternatives and intergroup relations. In H. Tajfel (ed.), *Differentiation Between Social Groups*. London: Academic Press.

Turner, J. C. and Giles, H. (1981). *Intergroup Behaviour*. Oxford: Basil Blackwell.

Turner, J. H. (1982). *The Structure of Sociological Theory*. Homewood, Ill.: Dorsey Press.

Veitch, A. (ed.) (1981). *Naked Ape: An Anthology of Male Chauvinism from the Guardian*. London: Duckworth.

Vroegh, K. (1971). Masculinity and femininity in the elementary and high school years. *Developmental Psychology, 4,* 254–61.

Ward, C. (1979). Differential evaluation of male and female expertise – prejudice against women? *British Journal of Social and Clinical Psychology, 18,* 65–9.

Warotamasikkhadit, U. (1967). Some phonological rules in Thai. *Journal of the American Oriental Society, 87* (4), 570–3.

Weinberg, B. and Bennett, S. (1971). Speaker sex recognition of 5 and 6-year-old children's speech. *Journal of the Acoustical Society of America, 50,* 1210–13.

Weinreich, U. (1963). *Languges in Contact,* The Hague: Mouton.

Weller, G. and Bell, R. O. (1965). Basal skin conductance and neonatal state. *Child Development, 36,* 647–57.

Wells, G. (1979). Variation in child language. In V. Lee (ed.), *Language Development.* London: Croom Helm.

White, A. and Wood, V. (eds) (1982). *Naked Ape 2: An Anthology of Sexism Collected by the Guardian.* London: Duckworth.

Wiggins, J. S. (1979). A psychological taxonomy of trait-descriptive terms: The interpersonal domain. *Journal of Personality and Social Psychology, 37* (3), 395–412.

Wiggins, J. S. (1980). Circumplex models of interpersonal behaviour. In L. Wheeler (ed.), *Review of Personality and Social Psychology.* Beverly Hills: Sage, 265–94.

Wiggins, J. S. (1982). Circumplex models of interpersonal behaviour in clinical psychology. In P. C. Kendall and J. N. Butcher (eds), *Handbook of Research Methods in Clinical Psychology.* New York: John Wiley.

Wiggins, J. S. and Holzmuller, A. (1978). Psychological androgyny and interpersonal behavior. *Journal of Consulting and Clinical Psychology, 46* (1), 40–52.

Wiggins, J. S. and Holzmuller, A. (1981). Further evidence on androgyny and interpersonal flexibility. *Journal of Research in Personality, 15,* 67–80.

Williams, J. A. and Giles, H. (1978). The changing status of women in society: An intergroup perspective. In H. Tajfel (ed.), *Differentiation Between Social Groups: Studies in the Social Psychology of Intergroup Relations.* London: Academic Press, 431–46.

Williams, J. E. and Best, D. L. (1977). Sex stereotypes and trait favourability on the adjective check list. *Educational and Psychological Measurement, 37,* 101–11.

Williams, J. E., Giles, H., Edwards, J., Best, D. L. and Daws, J. T. (1977). Sex trait stereotypes in England, Ireland and the United States. *British Journal of Social and Clinical Psychology, 16,* 303–9.

Wish, M., D'Andrade, R. G. and Goodnow, J. E. (1980). Dimensions of interpersonal communication: Correspondences between structures for speech acts and bipolar scales. *Journal of Personality and Social Psychology, 39* (5), 848–60.

Witkowski, S. R. and Brown, C. H. (1977). An explanation of color nomenclature universals. *American Anthropologist, 79,* 50–57.

Wolfram, W. (1969). *A Sociolinguistic Description of Detroit Negro Speech.* Washington, DC: Center for Applied Linguistics.

Wolfram, W. and Fasold, R. W. (1974). *The Study of Social Dialects in American English.* Englewood Cliffs, NJ: Prentice-Hall.

Wolfson, N. and Manes, J. (1980). Don't 'Dear' Me! In S. McConnell-

Ginet, R. Borker and N. Furman (eds), *Women and Language in Literature and Society*. New York: Praeger, 79–92.

Wood, M. (1966). The influence of sex and knowledge of communication effectiveness on spontaneous speech. *Word, 22* (1, 2, 3), 112–37.

Worell, J. (1978). Sex roles and psychological well-being: Perspectives on methodology. *Journal of Consulting and Clinical Psychology, 46* (4), 777–91.

Zimmerman, D. H. and West, C. (1975). Sex roles, interruptions and silences in conversation. In B. Thorne and N. Henley (eds), *Language and Sex: Difference and Dominance*. Rowley, Mass.: Newbury House.

Zimmerman, D. H. and West, C. (1978). Male–female differences in patterns of interruption and responses to interruption in two-party conversations. Paper read at Ninth World Congress of Sociology, Sweden.

Index of Names

Index of Subjects